RELATIONSHIP RESET

RELATIONSHIP RESET

SECRETS FROM A COUPLES THERAPIST THAT
WILL REVOLUTIONIZE YOUR LOVE FOR A LIFETIME

JEN ELMQUIST

MA, LMFT

Printed in the United States of America

To

FM
Trustsquare
&
Seven Generations

Contents

ACKNOWLEDGMENTS   **IX**

INTRODUCTION   **XIII**

1. A Little Explanation   1

CORE ELEMENTS:

THINK LIKE A COUPLES THERAPIST   **7**

2. Cycles—The Couples Journey   9
3. Patterns—Drama to Durable   49
4. Styles—All Couples Fight   89
5. Lesson from Viktor   109

MIND BENDERS:

BE THE CHANGE IN YOUR RELATIONSHIP   **117**

6. Stopping the Train   119
7. A Loving Observer   127
8. The Small Big Things   133
9. Releasing Expectations   137
10. Becoming More Critical   141
11. Relational Accounting 101   147
12. Three Positives   155
13. Clean Slate Protocol   159

MUSCLE BUILDERS:
CREATE A STRONG CONNECTION   **163**

14. The Epic Kiss   165
15. "Can You Hear Me?"   169
16. Let's Get It On   175
17. Vision Quest   183
18. Say a Little Prayer for Me   189
19. Getting the Whole Picture   195
20. Keep It Interesting   201
21. What about You?   207
22. The Research Project   213

CONCLUSION: A SWAN STORY   **223**
RELATIONSHIP RESET PLEDGE   **230**
RESEARCH AND RESOURCES   **231**
INDEX   **241**
ABOUT THE AUTHOR   **253**

Acknowledgments

A few years back, I received an email from a woman named Sarah. Sarah was on a couples retreat planning committee at Lake Harriet United Methodist Church (LHUMC) in Minneapolis. She had found my website, liked what she read, and wanted to know if I would be willing to lead a retreat. I emailed her back and said, "Thank you for the compliment, but I don't lead couples retreats. Best of luck to you!" You see, at that time, I thought, "I don't lead couples retreats. I run a private practice with a caseload of couples, teach couples therapy to graduate school students, and supervise students learning to practice couples therapy, but retreats?" Why I couldn't connect the dots now makes me laugh. The next year, I received the same email from Sarah. Once again, she was planning their annual couples retreat and was wondering if I would lead it. This time, it all made sense to me—maybe if I lead a retreat, I can get to couples before they need to see a couples therapist. Eureka! That was the year *Relationship Reset* was born. This book would not exist if Sarah had not been persistent and called me forward. I am so grateful for her and the couples from LHUMC that helped *Relationship Reset* come to be.

The development of this book was built on decades of study and practice in the field of relationships and through the gift of being in a committed relationship with an amazing guy. My partner, Jess

Elmquist, has been essential in the creation of *Relationship Reset*. Not only has he encouraged me every step of the way and agreed to share our story, but he has also jumped in, lending his personal expertise to this project. Over the last twenty-five years, Jess has become an in-demand master teacher and coach, currently running a corporate university that hires and trains over twenty-six thousand employees internationally. He is innovative and accomplished when it comes to instructing and inspiring people. He worked through each of the exercises in this book to make sure that they would facilitate couples learning together. Without his help, this book would not be complete. And well beyond any professional contribution, I love the life we have built together with our children. Thank you to my family, my Trustsquare; you are my people, and if I could save time in a bottle, I would save every moment to spend with you.

Much of what I have learned about couple relationships has come from the couples that bravely sought out therapy, believing there was a better way to live and love together. Sitting with their pain and hope taught me that all people just want to be loved well. This book was written with their stories and that desire in mind. Also, I would never have put the pieces of this book together without the privilege of being a teacher. My time at Saint Mary's University of Minnesota with inspiring colleagues and students has been transformative. I believe I have learned more than I have ever taught and made valuable relationships along the way. One such relationship began in a summer session of a class called Couple Relationships. I remember like yesterday a bright, energetic woman who filled the class with wisdom beyond her years. Thanks to that class, I got to know Marissa Bader and had the honor of being a part of her graduate school journey. She returned the favor and joined me on the journey of writing *Relationship Reset*. Before graduate school, Marissa was a writer, journalist, and editor. She offered me those skills, along with the lens of a marriage and family therapist, to help craft this book into existence. I will be forever thankful for all she has taught me.

Encouragement is an essential catalyst to purpose. Without the support of some significant people, I would never have had the confidence to pursue the important things in my life. To me, these people are angels, beings that show up at just the right time with the right message. My gratitude for their presence in my life is vast. Thank you to my angels: Janiece Greupner, Fred Rogers, Ert Hermerding, Kathy Bruner, Phil Frazier, Jim Moline, Susan Wehmann, Karen Covell, Paula Vento, Steve McManus, Steve Peltier, Sara Wright, Mark Flaten, and Ann Scott-Dumas. Thank you to my lady friends—the ones who have kept me grounded and laughing: Alicia, Lisa, Heather, Kerry, Angie, Di, Mo, Mick, Shari, Karen, Sara, Diana, Cara, and my true sister, Laura Lee. And thank you to my family of origin, specifically: my brother, E—you are truly a gift from God; my dad and mom, for your love and persistence in the things that matter; and my grandparents, for the joy and stability you provided throughout the years.

Finally, to all who have dedicated their life work to being a healing presence in the world, I extend extreme gratitude. You inspired me. As a result, I became a shoulder scholar, meaning everything I know came from the brilliant and talented people who let me stand on the shoulders of their knowledge to catch a new view. Hopefully, as you read through this book, you will be introduced to many of them and will find reference to their fantastic efforts in the Research and Resources section at the end. If their thoughts interest you, I encourage you to pick up their books, visit their websites, or attend their events.

To you, the reader, thank you for taking the time to think and grow with me. There are so many ways you can spend your moments; I am grateful for the moments you will spend with *Relationship Reset*. May it *Revolutionize Your Love for a Lifetime*!

Introduction

Nothing creates a greater imprint on our hearts and souls than our intimate connections. Through moments of great joy to those of deep pain, the couple relationship informs and defines our existence. Different from any other relationship experience we have during our time on earth, it is the one we can long for until we find it, take for granted when we have it, find security in as we grow through it, and take comfort in as we age. It holds power through its vast expressions of love, yet remains a life work for most to figure out how to make this mysterious pairing satisfying for a lifetime.

Once a couple makes the commitment to be together long term or for life, they enter into a unique process of development not otherwise experienced in other relationships. This experience initiates enormous growth for both partners, which makes it challenging. At least, that is what lifelong, committed relationships are for most people. Finding the balance that keeps us connected, energized, passionate, and productive day after day and year after year isn't easy. What ultimately defines the relationship happens in moments, the small hours that remain and hold us together or break us apart. The best of relationships have slumps, seasons of questions, points of doubt, and times of change. As a matter of fact, committing to the same person for a lifetime means having, at a minimum, four different relationships just due to changes in the typical family life cycle. And change is hard! There are three ways change affects couple relationships: First, change is a guarantee; there isn't a relationship out there that won't experience change and, in turn, be required to adapt and accommodate. Second, change is emotional as it asks us individually and as a couple to stretch beyond our comfort zones. And third, change is often resisted, as a couple fights to keep their relationship in a comfortable balance.

Then, beyond the impact of change, there are the common stressors of life every couple faces. I am certain you know what I am talking about—financial obligations and work priorities, life responsibilities and accountabilities, and the daily needs of family and friends all asking for your attention while you and your partner attempt to maintain individual and collective hopes and dreams. Keeping up with life together while also tending to a romance can be complex and messy. Many years are spent spread thin as partners each try to meet the demands of building and maintaining a shared world. On top of that, many couples are part of the growing number of people in the world who have bravely combined families. These couples have stepped into one of the most complicated love relationships to navigate. Finding time to nurture a new romantic relationship while also trying to merge two distinct families is nothing short of a miracle most days. There are so many challenges partners face together in the long-term, committed couple relationship, which is why at times everyone's relationship needs a *reset.*

Long-Term, Committed Relationship or Marriage?

Frankly, I don't want labels or language to get in the way of learning. If you have been tracking the political climate on relationships, you know the construct of marriage has faced unprecedented and long-overdue challenges in our culture. While the "right" associated with marriage has shifted, the choice to activate that "right" is facing delay or diminishing altogether. Today, according to the Pew Research Center report *5 Facts about Love and Marriage*, the desire to be in a married or committed relationship is high, with 75 percent of the US adult population reporting this desire. Simultaneously, the overall marriage rate has declined to the lowest point in America since the 1920s. Also, with the current marriage rate at roughly 50 percent of Americans over the age of eighteen, surprisingly, 70 percent of Americans would say they are in a committed couple relationship.

Renegotiating the constructs of commitment is a typical historical occurrence. Stephanie Coontz covers this topic extensively in her book *Marriage, a History*, highlighting how love relationships over the centuries have been defined and redefined time and again. Whether the relationship is constructed through formal legal contracts, spiritual or religious sanction, a couple's sincere intention, or all three doesn't change the journey. So however you define your contract, if you are in a lifelong, committed couple relationship, this book is for you.

Why Relationship Reset?

Relationship Reset is meant to help you engage with your partner in new ways, invigorate your life together, and create a revolution in your relationship. Your relationship can improve radically through gaining insight into what is "normal" in couple relationships, working individually on your contributions to the relationship, and finally, growing connections that give strength for longevity and sustainability. The simple tools in this book can make a difference and *do* work.

How do I know that? For the last decade, I have extensively studied couple relationships, taught couples therapy to graduate school students, and worked in private practice with couples just like you, helping them revive their relationships and find new levels of satisfaction. During that time, I was disturbed by a statistic from Dr. Clifford Notarius that reports *the average couple is unhappy for up to six years before seeking professional help.* Yikes! Six years is a long time to feel unsure about your partner or to be struggling in your relationship. And I found this to be true as couples would come into my office in rough shape, so emotionally worn down by their problems that the task of learning new ideas and implementing new skills felt incredibly daunting. Often I thought, "I wish people knew sooner what a couples therapist knows; then they could become experts on their relationship. With that knowledge they could hit reset before it was too late."

So, that is why I built *Relationship Reset*: to deliver knowledge, support, and tools to couples before it is too late. And also because, truth be told, most couples will never see a couples therapist. Why? Well . . .

"You Have to Be Crazy to Go to Therapy"

I have heard, "You have to be crazy to go to therapy" so many times; there is a stigma that a person must have some significant problems if he or she needs to see a therapist. This stigma is one of the main obstacles to couples getting support early on when their problems are still manageable. I have also heard people say, "People only go to couples therapy when they are going to break up." This idea has some validity, because by the time most couples get to therapy, they are so beat up in their relationship that often the only solution that seems reasonable is to be done. These common opinions aside, therapy also requires two things people find scarce: time and money. It is increasingly difficult to afford to see a couples therapist, and so when people do come, it is in crisis. I liken this experience to the way we deal with our physical health. If we have a cold, we still go about our daily business and press through. But if we have cancer, our world stands still, and we spare no expense to find health. When couples come to therapy in crisis, they have realized there is cancer in the relationship they have to address. It is only when the relationship is facing a terminal threat that couples clear their calendars and open their wallets. But the reality is, it is so hard to reset your relationship once it is in crisis. I wish the couples that came to see me had this information years earlier. So for all of you out there who are *not* going to see a couples therapist, at least not now anyway, you need this information today.

On a more personal level, this book is also crafted out of the knowledge my partner, Jess, and I have gained after weathering the waves of twenty-five-plus years together. After spending a long time in a committed relationship, there are nuggets of wisdom that come as rewards for doing the hard time. Initially, my instinct was to keep the personal stuff private. After all, I have observed a lifetime worth of valuable lessons in my work and study of other couples. But the truth is, if I can't show you how I have authentically lived what I am writing, there will be a missing piece in this book. You will find our story in the conclusion and hear how, by doing the very suggestions offered to you in *Relationship Reset*, we created a revolution in our relationship. You need to know you are not alone, and if anything we have learned can benefit you, it is well worth sharing our story. Isn't that why we are all here together, to help each other out and lift each other up to a more abundant life? Jess and I believe relationships matter. Your relationship matters. And if we can encourage and inspire you, then our joy is made complete.

Here's the Good News!

Not only is this book built off a lifetime of relationship experience and informed by years of study on relationships, but it also contains the same information most couples therapists will give you in their office. After you are done reading *Relationship Reset*, you will be thinking like a couples therapist and looking at your relationship through the same lens that someone trained to work with couples uses to make relationships better. And because you are reading this book, I am assuming you would like to have a better relationship. That is wonderful because it implies you are motivated. Even the motivation of one partner can make a significant impact on relationship satisfaction. One of the benefits of the experience in this book is that many activities don't require both partners to participate to instigate positive change. Maybe you are ready to have a better relationship, but your partner isn't quite on the same page yet. You can take these ideas and implement them into your relationship immediately, without waiting for your partner to jump onboard. How lucky, however, if both of you are committed to working together. Setting an intention to change your relationship together will create a revolution in your relationship. One of the best indicators of a relationship headed for success is alignment. When couples can get on the same page, set goals, and then achieve them together, it creates an unstoppable bond. So either way, together or on your own, *Relationship Reset* will impact your relationship for the better.

Warning: Your Relationship Could Look Radically Different When You Are Done Reading This

The information in this book is essential for couples to have a healthy, thriving relationship. Not only will you receive research-based insights, but you will also be equipped with tried-and-tested tools that work. One of the critical elements of any growth is the ability to take what you learn and easily apply it with repetition to experience real and sustainable change. To set you and your relationship up for success, *Relationship Reset* provides you with cutting-edge knowledge along with simple reset actions for you to experiment with in your relationship. The actions have been ordered to give you the greatest benefit while strategically offering steps that build on one another. However, if you read through and there is an action that speaks to your relationship today, start there! You can always go back for the rest later. Also, you may feel so overwhelmed with your life that the thought of doing multiple actions is just too much to handle. I would encourage you to pick the one that seems most doable and start there. Getting started is the key. Momentum follows action!

So, Let's Get Started!

Before you dig in, remember this: *commitment* is crucial. I know you are capable of commitment, or you wouldn't be reading this. There was a very special day at one point in your relationship when you both looked at each other and declared an *intention* to be together. By reading *Relationship Reset*, you are once again saying there is something special in this relationship. So, this is another time where you can *intentionally commit* to your relationship. Four attitudes will make all the difference if adopted before doing the work in this book. Those attitudes are Alignment, Reciprocity, Trust, and Love. Here is a short description of how each attitude helps foster an environment for positive change in your relationship:

- *Attitude of Alignment* is being committed to finding ways to get on the same page together. You may not be in the same sentence or even paragraph, but getting on the same page means you're both in this together. It is as simple as agreeing to commit actively to the experience in this book, wholeheartedly, until you are done.

- *Attitude of Reciprocity* means each of you is equally engaged in the process and giving 100 percent. The path to success is illuminated when both partners take responsibility and don't leave each other hanging. This means that both of you will read, discuss, try the exercises, and complete the work without being cajoled, manipulated, prompted, or parented by your partner.

- *Attitude of Trust* seeks to build a safe place where each of you can be honest and vulnerable. This can only happen if you have your partner's back and are keeping his or her best interest at heart. Ultimately, trust resides in the collective belief that the only way we win is together.

- *Attitude of Love* is based on the actions of being committed to love, not just the feelings of falling in love. When two people are committed to love each other, they treat each other justly and with kindness, mercy, and grace. This is crucial as you are trying something new, because it creates an environment where you can make mistakes and still be secure in your relationship.

Adopt these attitudes and then really sink in and give yourself wholly to the *Relationship Reset* experience. In the end, I believe you will experience a *revolution* in your relationship!

1

A Little Explanation

The best relationship problem solvers have the unique ability to synthesize large amounts of information while simultaneously rifling through a big catalog of solutions to address the issues in front of them. As I was mapping out the best way to approach the myriad of concerns that couples have about their relationships, I used this problem-solving procedure to come up with an order of actions that build on each other while also providing effective solutions that can benefit every couple. You see, I get it—no two relationships are alike. There is no way that one book is going to address the very specific needs your relationship has; however, I also know that there are universal insights and actions that offer positive results across the board for all couple relationships. That said, you will find *Relationship Reset* organized into three strategic sections to provide the most positive impact on your relationship: First, there are the Core Elements, which normalize what's going on in most relationships and get you thinking like a couples therapist. Then come the Mind Benders to expand your relational mind and help each partner become better attuned to the relationship. And finally are the Muscle Builders, which show you how to increase your couple connection and add strength to your relationship. Let's take a look at what each of these categories contains.

Core Elements

"Is this normal?" Due to a highly sensitive, inclusive approach to the world these days, most therapists avoid this question like the plague. The last thing they want to be on the line for is defining "normal" for any client. And while this is understandably admirable, sometimes people just need the reprieve that comes from someone saying, "Yep—I have seen this a million times," or "You know what? What you're dealing with is not very common." There is a particular relief provided by being able to categorize our fears, symptoms, issues, and concerns into a box that says, "You can let it go," or a box that says, "You need to give this more attention."

That is the purpose of the first section explaining the Core Elements. This section covers the couples journey through the Six-Stage Change Cycle of Committed Couple Relationships and what the common experiences are in each stage; Relationship Patterns and the way couples learn to dance with each other over the years; and Conflict Styles, the permanent presence of conflict in every relationship and how to become a Humble Warrior.

The Core Elements are fundamental and important ways to normalize what is going on in your relationship to put your concerns in context. Once you can normalize where your relationship is and how it operates, you will establish a baseline. This baseline will allow you to move into the remaining sections with clarity about what actually constitutes a problem and what doesn't, defining where to best put your effort toward improvement. It is amazing how many couples stay stuck and focused on issues in a relationship that are just normal relationship stuff. A little bit of insight can save a whole lot of pain and agony, which can often get stretched out and grow worse over the years.

Mind Benders

Mind over relational matter matters. The power of our personal, inner emotional world has the greatest influence on the success or failure of our intimate relationships. This claim is bold but scientifically accurate. Ultimately, what we believe affects how we think, which affects how we feel, which in turn affects how we act. In the most rudimentary sense, this is the basis for cognitive behavioral therapy, developed by psychiatrist Aaron T. Beck, which works with the inner world of an individual to change their external experiences. This process is called self-regulation. The ability to self-regulate well has a wealth of confirmed research linked to relational satisfaction across the board. The power of self-regulation has been made enormously popular in Daniel Goleman's emotional intelligence movement and by our modern-day reintroduction to ancient mindfulness practices. Being able to manage and communicate your inner emotional experience clearly has significant benefits to our personal health and the ability to have an optimal function in life.

Also, increased self-regulation is the key to enhancing your couple relationship. Consider this: If your mind is running wild about your relationship, your emotions are too. And out-of-control emotions are guaranteed to create dissatisfaction and discontentment. The Mind Benders in *Relationship Reset* help you elevate your mind in your relationship, increasing your self-regulation. These actions alone have the unique ability to shift the relationship in significant ways without your partner having to change with you. Then, beyond your individual work, you will find that when you work on your minds together, it creates what most relationships are begging for: better communication.

Muscle Builders

Going the distance as a couple requires building strength in the relationship. After normalizing your relationship experiences and teaching you how to adjust your mind to benefit one another, it is essential to increase the strength of your connection. In my couples therapy office, I always have enough seats for four people: one for each partner, one for myself, and one for the relationship. As you most likely have come to understand in your experience, relationships become their own entity. Just like having a child or starting a business, at one point what begins as an excellent idea eventually grows up and develops its own personality, demands, needs, habits, problems and successes. It becomes a living, breathing, stand-alone emergence of idea in action. If given proper care and attention, the benefits are endless. If ignored or neglected, the outcome is detrimental.

Relationships are the same way—they aren't meant to go from idea to action and then just coast on for years. There isn't a relationship that can thrive that way. Instead, just like being a loving parent or reliable business partner, the relationship needs the couple to build it up. It requires strong muscles to create a sustainable trajectory toward health and longevity. *Relationship Reset* offers Muscle Builders that work specifically on increasing the strength of your relationship.

Once you learn the Core Elements, Mind Benders, and Muscle Builders, you will be a well-equipped relationship expert with a deeper and more insightful view of yourself, your partner, and your relationship than you have had before. And isn't a relationship expert what we should all strive to become when it comes to our most precious and intimate connections? So often we take for granted that this relationship has appeared in our world, but I urge you to take a minute to marvel at the mystery. Out of billions of people, the two of you found each other, connected, and committed. What an incredible gift life has delivered to your feet! We treat this relationship with the respect it deserves when we decide to become students of our committed relationships. So put on your thinking caps; it is time to get to work.

CORE ELEMENTS

Think Like a Couples Therapist

Everything we buy these days has a manual that describes how the item works and how to troubleshoot problems if and when they arise. The Core Elements are a foundational manual for committed couple relationships, helping partners to understand normal function, what kind of problems might come up, and ideas on how to troubleshoot. Each Core Element highlights usual experiences that all couple relationships face with the intention of creating greater insight into your personal experiences.

2

Cycles—The Couples Journey

Before going on any journey, it is highly advised that you know where you are currently and where you are headed. There isn't a GPS out there that can give you directions without a current location and a destination. Mapping your journey as a couple is equally as important. All committed relationships have stages of development, and if you know what stage your relationship is in, it becomes much easier to define what is normal versus what is a problem. So often we get discouraged in our relationships because we confuse normal relationship experiences with problems. A lot of couples assume their unions are in distress when really they are just experiencing the typical growing pains that all people's relationships endure.

Like human beings, every relationship has its own life cycle. Similar to the way people go through different development stages and evolve over time, relationships do too. For instance, in the most traditional way, every new couple must adjust to living life as a team of two; couples may then decide they want to have children, and navigate the transitory and challenging period of welcoming little ones into the family system; and eventually, a couple's children will move out, leaving partners to readjust to life as a team of two again. These are very normal life transitions that create big changes and significantly affect the relationship.

Beyond couple and family life transitions, each partner goes through his or her own stages of lifespan development, which ultimately affect the relationship too. From birth to death, we are constantly growing and evolving. As we continue to understand more about ourselves through the years, we also continue to learn how to share ourselves with other people. This may be the most rewarding, yet difficult, task of our lifetime. It is no wonder that when we are involved in an intimate relationship for an extended period of time, we tend to see the largest growth curve; navigating our personal development while trying to stay in sync with another changing being is the "hard work" people associate with long-term, committed relationships. If you think about it, the standard marriage vows that have been uttered by millions over the centuries are, in essence, promoting the promise to commit to changing with one another. Have you heard this before? "I, (name), take you, (name), to be my partner, to have and to hold from this day forward, for better, for worse, for richer, for poorer, in sickness and in health, to love and to cherish until death do us part." These vows are saying that when life brings changes that affect us, which life inevitably always does, we will not only hang in there with each other until the end of time, but we will commit to continuously change with one another and do so with love. This is a *huge* promise to make to another human being. If you have made this promise, you are remarkable.

However, here's the problem: These changes often show up unexpectedly, and with them comes the inextricable byproduct of individual personal growth. And when we change as individuals, our relationships have to change, too. It is the complexity of personal development that upsets relationships and asks us to reevaluate and find each other again. Tragically, this is often when many couples become convinced that something is wrong with their relationship rather than understanding that they are in the midst of change. As a result, they may decide the relationship wasn't meant to be or that something is wrong with their choice of partner, instead of realizing that they can actually embark on a new relationship with the same person.

As a couples therapist, I have seen some of the greatest relief in partners when they finally understand that the conflict and discomfort they have been enduring are shared experiences stemming from natural relationship changes. As you take a look at the Six-Stage Change Cycle of Committed Couple Relationships, hopefully you too will feel a sense of relief when you come to understand your experiences on the couples journey.

Six-Stage Change Cycle of Committed Couple Relationships

The Six-Stage Change Cycle is derived from understanding couple life-span development in conjunction with the ongoing adult identity development process. Influenced by the ideas and theories of past and present scholars, I have created a change model that highlights a couple as a dynamic, organic, and transforming system while also explaining the typical, everyday experiences partners go through individually and together. In the field of marriage and family therapy, there can never be enough attempts at encapsulating the process of the couple relationship. This is helpful not only for therapists, but also especially for couples like you who are trying to become experts on their own relationships. And that is precisely my hope in sharing this model with you; I want you to become an expert on your relationship. In turn, this will help you understand why it can, at times, be so challenging to grow with someone you love so much.

I'd like to offer a little background on what I mean by this. As I mentioned earlier, as humans, we begin growing and developing in relationships the minute we are born. Attachment theory, pioneered by John Bowlby and Mary Ainsworth, tells us that way back in the beginning, even as infants, we were already being primed to love in adulthood. We learned early on how to bond with another human being through our relationship with our primary caregiver(s). Some of us may have had excellent teachers in our families who met our physical and emotional needs while tenderly offering us love and connection. Through our interactions with these caregivers, we learned how to attach to people in a secure way. Others may have had caregivers who were not as capable of bonding with and caring for us in the same healthy manner. This likely created an outcome of an avoidant or anxious attachment with others. The good news, however, is that most humans are enormously resilient and will continue to strive to create secure attachments throughout life, specifically in our most intimate, committed couple relationships. It is the construct of this partnership that remodels the initial childhood bond, giving us multiple opportunities to practice secure and connected love in adulthood.

The Six-Stage Change Cycle will help you see how we practice creating security in our relationships and why the couple relationship gets challenged more as we move through some of the stages as opposed to others. You will also learn how these stages correlate with transitions throughout the lifespan—times that often generate prime opportunities for us to become more confident and stable in a relationship with ourselves, others, and the world around us. Beyond that, you may identify with why couples get stuck in this cycle of change and how at times the changes or resistance of changes can cause relationships to end.

The Cycle Explained

The Six-Stage Change Cycle includes (1) You and Me, (2) We, (3) I and I, (4) The We/I Plateau, (5) The D-Factor, and (6) Us or Me. In just a moment, you will read in detail how each of these stages is defined and how they may express their presence in your relationship. However, it is important to understand that these stages are always cycling throughout the course of your relationship, and this is not necessarily a one-time, linear experience. Also, this cycle will look different for everyone. While you may find similarities with a friend or family member, each relationship cycles through the stages based on the uniqueness that each individual brings to the relationship, of which the combinations are endless. Some people may find that they have been through all of the stages in a short period of time, while others may find that they have stayed in a particular stage for an extended period of time. There is no right or wrong. The important piece to understand is that this change cycle does occur, and when it does, it often brings an uncomfortable transition to the relationship that can be perceived as a problem rather than normal growth.

You will be able to read through the definitions of each stage. This will allow you an in-depth understanding of how your relationship may respond to joint and individual changes over the years. I will review with you the indications that this change cycle may be undermining your relationship, and when it may be time to seek additional support. Also, we will look at the assets each stage offers the relationship long term. Next, I will cover challenges that the stages create and how you can navigate through them. Finally, you will have the opportunity to look at how the stages fit into the life cycle of the relationship and assess which stage or stages apply to your relationship. This last step will allow you to determine what is normal for your relationship and which areas of your relationship may need more attention as you continue to grow as a committed couple.

Stage One—You and Me (Attaching)

In old Hollywood film terms, this stage is the "meet-cute" when a couple, destined to be together forever, connects for the very first time. In this classic movie moment, you meet an amazing person, you are drawn to each other immediately, and the rest of the world fades away. You're totally enthralled with one another. Their look, smell, sound, touch, and thoughts are in perfect unison with yours. Isn't it amazing that you have found each other? There is no one else you would prefer to be with and you are willing to do just about anything to be together. The sexual connection is hot; as a matter of fact, a look can be just as charged as an orgasm. Decisions tend to be less complicated and often happen quickly. Passion rules at this point as you give in to a process referred to as "falling" in love. There are emotional and physiological chemical processes that help bond the connection while also suspending critical thinking. This is the beginning of love, often mistaken for "real love feelings." "Real love" actually develops throughout the change cycle, but this experience is an emotional set point that can be crucial down the road. Couples in this passionate meeting move from dating to commitment, creating the environment for the next stage in the relationship.

There are a variety of common experiences that rule this stage as each individual seeks to put their "best self" forward. For instance, personal hygiene is a high priority; it's important to shower, wear clean clothes, have fresh breath, clean up your home, and control bodily functions. As relationships move forward, partners may become more relaxed about some of these things, but initially, there is high vigilance on presentation of self. Not only is the physical presentation controlled, but so is our emotional presentation. Couples may find themselves moving between vulnerability and self-preservation as they weigh their emotional safety. This means that sometimes there are "spill your guts" moments, and other times important emotional details are withheld out of fear of sharing too much too soon. It is also common that you might engage in activities or experiences that your "not falling in love" self wouldn't usually do. This could include sitting through an event that bores you but your partner really likes, such as a baseball game, ballet performance, or poetry reading. If you typically like to sleep in on the weekends, you may find yourself waking up early because that is what your new partner likes. Even more unusual may be your participation in adventurous experiences you would normally turn down because they scare you to death, such as scaling great heights, like rock climbing, or going to great depths, like scuba diving.

Often couples in Stage One experience intense and intentional communication with a hyper focus and complete, rapt interest in their partner's thoughts and feelings. Think about your time spent in this stage: There is frequent and attentive calling and texting when you're not together, and when you are together, the hours may fly by without notice as you cover a broad range of topics. Often you are surprised by what you are willing to talk about and are excited by all the things you share in common. Most notable in this stage is the charged sexual connection, marked by the fact that you can't keep your hands off each other. New couples may enjoy major make-out sessions to frequent and spontaneous sex. This not only extensively bonds the relationship, but also creates a "love goggle" effect as the chemical exposure of oxytocin increases the illusion of perfection in our partner and temporarily suspends our judgment. The intense communication and sexual connection give rise to strong visions of a future together. Putting the other partner first with your time, thoughts, and emotions are an easy task. Rescheduling guys' or girls' nights out is no problem, your endorphins allow you to stay up all night before a big meeting and still succeed, and—oops! —you accidentally forget your mom's birthday. It happens. After all, you are in love. But, (downer alert), over focus on the relationship to the exclusion of other life priorities can create problems. These are things you need to look out for in Stage One:

- Your friends and family members may wonder if you are still alive and complain about you not having the time and attention for them that you had in the past. Work may not be the top priority, and it isn't unusual to be distracted or unable to concentrate.

- The illusions that being in love brings can cause you to miss significant obstacles or differences that can cause relationship problems down the road. The love goggles may distort the fact that he is always late or is really impatient with the waiter, and she never has anything out of place in her apartment or talks incessantly about her work. Maybe these behaviors are endearing at the beginning, but down the road they may become really annoying.

- This stage can create relationship expectations that will not be sustainable outside of this phase. From this vantage point, couples may assume that the hot, passionate sex will last indefinitely, that the priority of being together won't be challenged, or that moving in together will be a piece of cake. Due to the fluid nature of the relationship early on, couples can establish an unrealistic vision of what life together long term will look like.

• It is not uncommon during this time for miscommunications to remain unresolved due to the fragility of creating conflict in a new relationship. Experiences such as seeing the text from his ex and never asking about it, or saying nothing when she is a half hour late to dinner can lie on the floor waiting to be picked up at a later stage. Be aware that just because you let the issue go now doesn't mean that it won't affect the relationship down the road.

• If this is a second or subsequent relationship and there are already children involved, the joys of falling in love can be counter-balanced by managing other people's resistance and feelings of disappointment, confusion, or anger. Other challenges that may arise include when to merge the new and existing relationships, early negotiations with your partner about sharing responsibilities, and time constraints on being together alone.

On the other hand, Stage One provides a sound foundation for the long-term sustainability of the relationship and gives great reason to celebrate. Here are some of the benefits that will enhance the relationship going forward:

X Stage One sets the critical chemistry in motion that binds the relationship together. The intimate connection that is ignited here will become the adhesive property that holds the relationship together as it propels through the next stages.

X Stage One builds the lust/love foundation for ongoing attraction throughout the relationship. The set point of "the man or woman I fell in love with" allows us to remember throughout the stages why we committed in the first place.

X   Stage One creates a place to aspire and return to down the road as you are seeking to once again experience the intensely physical, emotional, and psychological attachment that was there in the beginning.

Stage Two—We (Establishing)

In Stage Two, a couple moves from the "meet-cute" to becoming a "We" couple. (Think matching T-shirts, drinking the same drink, eating off of each other's plates, finishing each other's sentences, picking up each other's dry cleaning, walking the dog, signing mortgage papers, etc.) During this time, couples are establishing patterns or "ways of being together." Decisions are made together concerning where we live, responsibilities we share and the tasks they require, and how we negotiate boundaries financially, sexually, spiritually, relationally, and socially. A new, shared life together that never existed before we met begins to emerge. This stage is important to acknowledge because it solidifies the relationship beyond emotion and plants roots in each other's day-to-day realities. Establishing the "We" builds comfort and assurance that this is a relationship that will go the distance. It is the development of this stage that ultimately makes separation so difficult. This is also the stage that establishes the way we communicate with each other, how vulnerable we will be, and the level of intimacy and transparency we can tolerate. Success in developing these patterns is often precluded by our previous individual development, including self-differentiation, emotional regulation, attachment styles, and our family-of-origin modeling of intimate relationships.

Some common experiences emerge in Stage Two that further develop and solidify the long-term commitment and connection between partners. This is the primary time that public announcements and declarations regarding relationship exclusivity and commitment are declared. Ranging from changing one's social media status to "in a relationship" to a civil ceremony, wedding, or celebration of love, the couple outwardly secures their commitment. Along with the excitement of the new life that is being built, there can also be fear over the changes that this new life brings. These are the two faces of commitment that show up as couples yield to make space for one another. This can be observed through vacillating feelings and thoughts, such as one day thinking that buying a house together seems like an excellent idea, while the next day it looks really scary, or the classic feeling of "cold feet" some experience before getting married. This is normal. Making large joint purchases and merging two lives together is an enormous transition. In the beginning, everything from negotiating housing, to buying furniture, to divvying up closet space, to choosing the best toothpaste is serious business, while it will become business as usual down the road.

Beyond merging lives, couples also find themselves committing to shared responsibilities, such as being on the same phone contract, purchasing a pet together, or even building a business. By doing this, couples create a shared identity. This shared identity can be further expressed by being part of the same organizations and communities, like being a plus-one on an RSVP, joining the same running group, attending religious services together, or showing up weekly at the same coffee shop. Finally, the "We" couple ventures into the critical concept of togetherness when they consider family planning and the important step of introducing "new life" (children) into the relationship. This may come about in a variety of ways, from natural childbirth to adoption, to blending family systems, thus turning partners into parents. Upon doing so, they permanently bond their connection through the life of another human being, and regardless of what happens with their romantic union, they will be in a parenting relationship throughout the entire life of their child.

One important key to the long-term success of a couple can be found in their original motivations for becoming a "We". If couples slide into this stage without much thought, meaning they end up living together gradually because it makes their lives easier or for financial convenience, research indicates that durability of the commitment can be compromised. On the contrary, couples that are very intentional about combining their lives and make active, informed decisions about being together find that their success over the long haul is much higher. Furthermore, committing to a partner out of obligation, outside pressure, or external approval from others is a motivation that can fail over time. The best way to engage in Stage Two is through thoughtful consideration and intentional choice.

Although it is a really exciting time, this period also creates an environment for conflict as increased time together and close proximity of living coincide. As you navigate this territory, watch out for these landmines:

- Disagreements over how each partner likes to have things done or take care of tasks come up. The little things, from how the toilet paper roll is hung to whether shoes are on or off in the house, can create conflict.

- Differences in time management and prioritizing emerge. Is your partner a ten-minutes-early or ten-minutes-late kind of person? What comes first: work or play? These differences can cause frustration and arguments during this stage.

- Competing values can create conflict and are found at the

root of most couple issues. Value-driven disagreements may occur around finances, intimacy, leisure time, work and career, family, friends, living arrangements, personal habits, and parenting styles. Every one of these topics is bound to need intentional discussion for partners to come to a shared understanding.

• Difficulties in sharing arise as space and things are negotiated. Is anything off-limits for you, or do you need some specific type of privacy? Will you share closet space, have access to each other's phones and computers, or need a particular side of the bed? Issues like this are critical to consider and will demand attention.

Without the development of a "We" couple, there won't be an established long-term, committed relationship. This is where the relationship is forged, and the gifts given during this time of establishment and commitment make the relationship work. Consider the high value of what this stage brings by honoring what happens:

X Stage Two writes the "relationship contract": the rules and agreements of how this relationship will work. This is a living document that will go with you the distance of the relationship and be renegotiated in the years to come. If you are conscious of reevaluating the contract throughout the relationship, it can be a real asset.

X Stage Two develops boundaries that communicate where "You" start and "I" end, along with what's mine, what's yours, and what's ours. This is imperative because it helps manage conflict. It also is how you can understand your conflict in the future, because when people are upset, a boundary has usually been crossed.

X Stage Two establishes patterns that set the balancing point for the remainder of the relationship, defining how you are going to work with each other on all aspects of being together.

Stage Three—I and I (Individuating)

"I and I" moments begin once the bonded "We" couple feels the freedom to again focus on individual self-discovery and development. In Stage Three, partners start exploring personal pursuits with new energy, such as reinvesting in a current job for a promotion, pursuing different career options, engaging in education, exploring new hobbies, and/or working toward bucket-list goals. Partners do this with the stability of knowing that they have a secure relationship—a home base. Throughout this stage, partners may be very supportive of one another, or they might need to renegotiate how to balance "We" and "I" time in the relationship. Either way, this stage usually doesn't threaten the relationship, but instead vitalizes it by creating new individual energy and bringing some outside variety into the couple sphere.

In this stage, it is typical for individuals to become more self-focused rather than hyper-focused on each other, as in Stage One, or intensely "We" focused, as in Stage Two. Naturally, less time may be spent together as individuals in a relationship discover or rediscover their sole interests and passions. The relationship stability that was forged as couples created a solid "We" identity is critical here, as it allows individuals within a relationship to pursue their own interests and then share in and celebrate their accomplishments together.

Even though this time can be reenergizing, it also introduces the concept of competing priorities, which can cause problems for couples. For instance, one partner may be picking up the slack in order for the other partner to be successful, which can create resentment.

On the flip side, one partner may feel guilty about not being able to manage their regular responsibilities. Keeping the following things in mind can be really helpful:

- Negotiating time for individual pursuits versus relationship tasks is a typical couple conflict during this stage. It is important that you are talking through what each partner can do for the other, what sacrifices need to be made, how long this period will last, and what the shared rewards will be when it is all over.

- Tensions regarding power differences can rise due to the lack of equality, or perceived lack of equality, in the relationship. For example, this may become a problem if one person takes the time to go back to school while the other partner is providing the income to pay bills and expenses.

- A sense of missing each other and wanting more connection is normal when a partner is absorbed in a goal outside of "We." Sometimes greater efforts need to be made to arrange time for each other. Keep in mind that leaning into the small moments—a quick lunch or dinner rather than a lengthy date—may be good enough during this time period. Beyond that, finding ways to join in and support your partner can make the experience even better for both of you.

Necessary and impactful personal and couple development occurs during the "I and I" experience in the relationship. Such development not only keeps each individual growing and thriving, but also affirms the security of the couple bond as partners support each other's life goals and pursuits. The following contributions are critical going forward:

X Stage Three restores balance to the couple and helps keep the relationship interesting. After two stages of intense focus on the couple relationship, individuals get to rest in the security of a supportive home base. This support is often essential to increasing confidence, motivation, and greater belief in self.

X Stage Three fosters an appreciation for time together and respect for time apart. Healthy relationships require this give-and-take.

X Stage Three builds admiration and respect for your partner as you support and observe their accomplishments. Having pride in your partner can increase your commitment and attachment to each other.

X Stage Three allows for personal life goals to be met, preventing future regrets and resentments that could be attributed to the relationship. The best prevention of future resentment is action in the present.

Stage Four—The We/I Plateau (Stabilizing)

It is common for couples to spend many years on a plateau straddling Stages Two and Three. This is called the "We/I" Plateau. The "We/I" Plateau is really the meat of life together; it is when we balance our individual identities and personal pursuits with the connection and intimacy of family life. As children are added, couples may feel an increased connection and tension, as the "We" and "I" identities become more complex and demanding. This time often continues throughout raising and launching children, even extending into the "sandwich" years, a season when partners are caring for multiple generations at once. During this stretch a couple's adult children are starting careers and families, while their parents are aging, becoming dependent and in need of care. These comprehensive years of family life can be overwhelming and exhausting at times, leaving minimal space to enjoy each other's company.

However, for most couples, these are the years that stabilize life together—building a family, career, financial security, and community ties. Often illustrated as a montage in the movies, this period layers multiple moments into a rich story of life. Some common experiences rule the "We/I" Plateau as couples often feel like they are going through the motions with little time to focus on each other the way they used to. Life gets busy as Monday blurs into Friday overnight and you find yourself asking, "Where did the time go?" It can be hard to schedule a haircut, let alone a romantic night out together as a couple, and sleep is a coveted commodity. During this stage, many couples give birth to, raise, and launch children; begin, grow, and retire their careers; and join, establish, and change communities. Sprinkled throughout this span, of course, is the love and laughter that accompanies happy moments and celebrating milestones, along with the trials and tears of losses and disappointments.

Although this season of life brings a lot of joy, it is no wonder that the "We" couple exits the plateau feeling like they need to reacquaint themselves with each other. It is also not surprising that each individual exits this same season with renewed energy toward personal goals. As you will learn next, it is typical for individuals leaving this plateau to question who they are and who they want to be in and outside of the relationship. Therefore, this is a time that requires vigilance on your part if you desire to keep your relationship strong. Keep a lookout for the following typical concerns:

- Needs of others may often trump the needs of the couple as the romantic relationship gives way to the day-to-day tasks of doing life together. During this time, the demands of others can be louder than your love life, and it takes discipline and sacrifice to remember each other's needs.

• When you continuously put each other off and spend less time focused on your love life, you may lose sight of why you are still with your partner in the first place. This can make you vulnerable to meeting emotional or romantic needs outside of your relationship. If this occurs, turn back toward your partner before it's too late.

• As the momentum of the life you created together takes over, partners may suffer a loss of individual identity. As everyone else's needs rise, the connection with your personal identity can fade into the background. Spousal, parental, and career-focused identities are relevant but are not the totality of who you are. However, during this time, these roles can certainly feel like they define you.

• Tensions between "We" and "I" can increase conflict in the relationship as partners strive to find a balance between their lives together and individual autonomy.

• Boredom with the monotony of life can generate a desire for "something more" outside of the relationship. As partners become more predictable together, the yearning for some excitement or new energy can grow.

• High stress from too many responsibilities can take a toll on both physical and mental health. Reduced time to exercise and practice good self-care can cause weight gain, bad eating habits, and increased substance use, all of which can be detrimental to a relationship.

• Emerging unexpected problems, such as unemployment,

illnesses, accidents, and losses, can really throw couples curve balls during this time. Unpredictable events will push your relationship to the limits.

All of the craziness aside, most couples affirm that the "We/I" Plateau is really the fulfillment of the life they envisioned together during Stages One and Two. The following are the gifts that Stage Four bestows upon couples:

X Stage Four establishes the family that couples desire. This family may include children, pets, extended family, grandchildren, and/or a close family of friends that will help define couples for a lifetime.

X Stage Four creates communities for couples. From the neighborhoods they live in to the organizations they participate in to the companies they work for, important places put their markers on couples' lives.

X Stage Four produces all kinds of opportunities for couples to leave their legacies. During these years, the accomplishments made together and as individuals leave signatures on life and remind the world of our identities after we are gone.

X Stage Four fills a couple's albums of memories. This phase documents the years spent together, what we looked like, where we went, the people we knew, and how we lived.

X Stage Four fortifies couples' commitments to one another as the joy and pain of life seal the bond into a permanent hold. By this time, so much life has been lived together that when the viability of the relationship is questioned, the assets often outweigh the liabilities.

X Stage Four increases secure attachments because, over time, the power of consistency can remodel our inner beliefs about finding safety and trust in others.

Stage Five—The D-Factor (Differentiating)

The D-Factor stands for differentiation. Differentiation was originally defined by psychiatrist Murray Bowen and is really just a big word for how we develop a confident, well-defined identity. A typical way we develop our identity is by comparing ourselves to others in our world. We start to understand who we are by contrasting our similarities and differences with everyone from our family members and friends to larger social networks. Then, as our differentiation increases, the more comfortable we become maintaining our true self with others, rather than needing to comply with or rebel against them. Adolescence is the first time we experience the D-Factor in life in a significant way. Actually, it is one of the primary developmental tasks of our teenage years, and it manifests in all sorts of physical and emotional expressions. What happens for many people, though, is that this task is only partially completed at the end of adolescence. The rest of our identity development continues into adulthood and often accelerates as we connect in intimate relationships. These relationships, once again, create a family-like environment where we can push against each other as we contrast "who I am in this relationship" with "who I am outside of this relationship." Just like in adolescence, when we pushed against our parents to leverage our development, we now use our partner in a similar way.

Because this is a recycling experience, it affects relationships differently and at different times based on the identity-development work left for each individual. In my opinion, this is the basis for some couple theories that believe we commit to the person that will heal us. Odd but true, most intimate relationships are assets for healing and eventually trigger our biggest and oldest emotional identity wounds, asking us to confront them. For some people, it might be fear of abandonment, for some their personal value, for some the pain of rejection or betrayal, for some the need for approval, and for yet others, the sense of not being good enough. These are just some examples of the many different core identity concerns that we carry with us into adulthood and that our couple relationship may stir up. Stage Five is when we really wrestle with "Who am I?" versus "Who am I in this relationship?" We struggle as we ask if these two versions of ourself are still compatible.

Individual discomfort with life can be a common indication that the D-Factor is in motion. This can present as a general malaise or can be a particular dissatisfaction with the relationship. It is typically accompanied by a high motivation for change. Often the desired change can encompass broad categories of life, including vocational, relational, social, physical, financial, spiritual, and familial categories. Big ideas and/or dormant dreams start to surface, and desires to try new things with or without our partner give rise. This is different than the Stage Three experience of the developing "I and I," which was also focused on individual goals and accomplishments, because the D-Factor has deep roots in redefining one's identity, while the "I and I" stage focuses on enhancing one's identity. With the D-Factor may come feelings of "Who I am isn't the person I want to be," or "I always wondered if I could be or do ____."

Some of our greatest accomplishments come about during this stage, as individuals can soar to new heights in their careers, take on new challenges they only dreamt of in earlier years, or step outside comfort zones and risk it all to live a life they always believed they would. There are many ways the D-Factor can influence us; perhaps it propels us to start a business, go back to school, travel, move to a different part of the country or world, or explore new aspects of ourselves. It also may simply appear as isolated questions, resulting in expedient answers that create swift adjustments in a couple's life. This can minimize the overall impact on the couple relationship, although it will still require the relationship to adapt. For example, a partner may finally get fed up with a career that doesn't reflect his or her identity and take on a new career in a short period of time. Even though this is an isolated change, it still requires the couple to modify and adjust to the ending of one career, the beginning of a new career, and all of the personal alterations involved from time management, to new relationships, to financial outcomes.

The D-Factor can also create dramatic waves in a couple's relationship. This typically occurs when it is set off by a reconstruction in how the world looks to us, often following times of disillusionment. The D-Factor can by propelled by the loss of a job, the death of a parent, the ending of a business or career, the break-up of a friendship, the launching of children, or the altering perspective of time that accompanies midlife, all jarring paradigm shifts. As a result, some of our biggest relationship troubles can manifest during this stage. It is not unusual for there to be a change in relationships with friends and family members during this time as an individual questions who they have been in comparison to who they might want to become. Typical experiences can range from changing long-held beliefs or traditions to reconciling family-of-origin relationships to resolving buried painful experiences or previous traumas. Some partners may try to resolve identity questions externally by changing their looks through wardrobe or surgery, making prosperity purchases (think red sports car or a big house), or having an affair. These changes can create couple relationship problems as partners try on new identities that don't fit within the confines of the couple's original agreement.

Some of the questions that threaten the relationship during this stage can include "Is there another relationship that would be better for me?" "Would I prefer to be alone?" or "Is there another version of this relationship that we can find together?" A classic statement that tends to arise during this period is "I love you, but I don't think I am *in* love with you anymore." This is a telltale sign that someone is differentiating and using the relationship to leverage their identity development. It is also the prime indicator that the relationship is entering a season of significant change.

The D-Factor will positively or negatively affect the relationship depending on how flexible couples are in working together and how adaptable they are when the desired changes in the relationship tend to be one-sided and demand patience. As the season of differentiation takes flight, it is critical for partners to realize that being there for each other through the "dark night of the soul" will test their relationship and require they pay more—not less—attention to their commitment. If there is resistance to change during this time, the relationship will ultimately have two choices: to become rigid and stagnant, or to become chaotic and possibly blow up.

The person who is not going through the D-Factor experience may question the stability and/or intentions of his or her partner and wonder, "What is happening? This isn't the person I committed to or married," or "Is my partner going through a mid-life crisis?" It is tough to try to maintain a connection with a moving target, and the D-Factor represents a period of change that can feel confusing and scary. For both partners, frustrations may escalate because the balance of the relationship is being challenged in ways it hasn't been before. This is what William Bridges, author of *Transitions: Making Sense of Life's Changes,* refers to as a neutral zone in transition, when the old way of life together has ended and a new way of being together has not yet been realized. You could think of it as a wool sweater on a wet, naked body: terribly uncomfortable and you cannot get it off fast enough. In most cases of differentiation, time is the great remedy. Just like during adolescence, it takes time to answer these core questions about one's self and come to comfortable conclusions. Supporting your partner and creating space for his or her process while also being true to your own needs in the relationship can be difficult. The following are some general concerns to be aware of during this unpredictable period of fluctuation:

- Partners can become distant and distracted as they ponder their own existence and purpose. Also common during this time is for apathetic or nonchalant attitudes to develop regarding the relationship. Due to this detachment, feelings of insecurity can emerge for both partners, which may bring up old attachment wounds of rejection or disapproval.

- Partners may become covert and dishonest as they try to manage the relationship internally and question its validity. This makes space for betrayal and new attachment wounds within the relationship to occur.

- Partners may become explicit about their dissatisfaction with the relationship and consequently seek comfort outside of the relationship. This can increase conflict and build a tenuous environment.

- Partners may adopt significant temporary or permanent

changes to long-held beliefs and values.

• The relationship may become vulnerable to infidelities and divorce, particularly if partners feel their union is standing in the way of desired life changes. These risks increase the more partners resist desires for change and blame each other rather than turning toward each other, talking through the process, and supporting one another.

• Change is a big trigger for the onset of circumstantial depression and/or anxiety. It is normal to experience symptoms of depression and anxiety when life circumstances are unstable or difficult, particularly in our most intimate relationships. Be aware of this possibility and get some support.

The birth of anything new usually comes with a period of exhaustive waiting and then difficult labor, followed by an uncomfortable transition to a new world order. The D-Factor gives birth to new partners and fresh beginnings, thus allowing couples to understand the following concepts:

X Stage Five helps individuals clarify their personal identity and fulfill life purposes and goals, bringing an authenticity and complexity to life together.

X Stage Five generates normal adult development, which is inevitable and healthy in relationships. This development can be seen in both big and small ways over the years together.

X Stage Five may move relationships in positive directions and serve as the instigator to push couples beyond their comfort zones and out of stagnation.

X Stage Five often inspires couples to make overdue changes

that have long been discussed or dreamt of over the years. It brings action to idling ideas and voice to unspoken opinions.

X   Stage Five infuses new energy into relationships and stimulates creativity as partners learn to adapt to new versions of each other.

Stage Six—Us or Me (Integrating)

This final stage happens in micro and macro experiences throughout the relationship as couples ask the fundamental question, "Should I stay or should I go?" Believe it or not, this question isn't as threatening as it sounds, and we ask it more often than we think. It is a stabilizing question that reflects a normal and healthy decision-making process couples continuously go through when evaluating their commitment to each other. Sometimes this question is asked and answered quickly as couples cycle out of the "We/I" Plateau and assimilate their years together with life-cycle changes. Other times it follows the birthing process of the D-Factor and requires painful consideration for one or both partners. Ultimately, the answer to this question is what leads couples to decide to either end their union or move back into the change cycle stages with each other.

Every time partners choose each other once again, it creates a fresh start point as they reenter Stage One and bond with a renewed passion. Couples that choose to stick together often feel like they are in a new relationship with a known partner, creating a path for even deeper love and attachment. This is a profound experience that is ultimately the gift of longevity and perseverance, found after spending years growing together rather than apart. It is also the reward that comes after two people have drifted into different spaces only to reconnect and discover each other all over again.

On the flip side, Stage Six may also be the point of realizing that this relationship will not continue. This moves individuals back into a "me" place where they decide they want to be single or, perhaps, look to reenter the change cycle with a new partner. Two of the primary reasons that relationships ultimately end are due to resistance to change. Either differentiation is not allowed to occur or when it does occur, the change it brings cannot be integrated. Often you hear partners say at the end of a relationship, "He or she changed," "He or she wouldn't change," or "I grew out of the relationship." These are accurate statements as partners change. But even more on point is the fact that *the relationship couldn't adapt* to the individual changes.

Some of the hardest yet most valuable work occurs in Stage Six. Many couples have transcendent moments of transparency as serious conversations occur regarding the state of the relationship. A higher level of emotional and psychological vulnerability usually emerges as requests for change are made. Old desires and needs from the relationship may be communicated for the first time in years. There is an overall sense of "There is nothing to lose, so let's just put it all on the table." Often there is excitement over fresh opportunities as the couple starts a new relationship together. Along with that excitement, however, partners may also feel trepidation and unease about all the changes, along with fear about the sustainability of this new state going forward. However, couples have to push through the discomfort to find the potential for positive integration and the hope of a new day together. When attempting to rearrange an existing relationship, it is crucial to look out for the following challenges:

- Conflict can increase as partners resist unwanted change and renegotiate the original relationship contract. Think of this time as a second "informed proposal." With all of the intimate knowledge and familiarity you have on each other now, would you still say yes to a commitment with your partner? This is your opportunity to say yes once again, with your eyes wide open.

• Change can cause confusion and disorientation until it is accepted and integrated. Couples may feel on edge like they did at the beginning of their relationship, once again unsure of how they feel about each other. There can even be an awkwardness of being together that is surprising to reexperience.

• Couples may struggle to understand each other in this new relational place, and they will need to enhance their communication and interpersonal skills. The old habits that got them here will not be the habits that propel them to a new and better relationship.

• Once again, change can cause anxiety and/or depression. The uncertainty in this stage may trigger or prolong circumstantial mental and physical health troubles that will need attention and care.

• During this time, some couples may feel they need to separate. It is not unusual for one partner to feel that he or she cannot process the changes requested while living in such close proximity to their mate. A trial separation, or what Lee Raffel calls a "controlled separation" in her book *Should I Stay or Should I Go?*, may be necessary to help couples determine the pros and cons of staying together, versus ending their relationship. Divorce may also be discussed.

Overall, Stage Six can bring enormous gifts to the relationship and the priceless value of stability and long-term commitment. If couples can navigate this stage together, they will have the type of relationship that can actually be depended upon for better or for worse. For couples that enter this stage and find that it leads to a release from the commitment, there is also a new day to be pursued. These couples are on the brink of possibility *if* the learning that this commitment brought to each partner can be realized. There are high hopes that the next relationship, together or apart, will be that much better.

Celebrate the following gifts found in this final stage:

X Stage Six reestablishes and elevates the commitment in the relationship to a whole new level. Because both partners have reevaluated the relationship and once again intentionally chose to stay together, the relationship benefits from the depth of this recommitment.

X Stage Six creates a base of love that is only found in lifelong relationships with the same partner. The knowing of one another that comes from living years together and understanding each other with such intimacy is of great value and cannot be acquired any other way.

X Stage Six can dissolve a relationship that is not working and create space for partners to grow individually and move on. Although typically not desired, finding a way to bring healthy closure to a relationship that cannot be sustained can benefit both partners long term. Remember, endings are as important as beginnings.

X Stage Six allows couples that stay together to transition into a "new" relationship, bringing vitality and excitement back. With each cycle through the stages, a couple puts to bed one version of their life together and steps into an updated version that offers fresh adventure with familiar comfort.

Challenges

There are some challenges to working with the Six-Stage Change Cycle of Committed Couple Relationships.

We don't always move through these stages in tandem. Couple conflict often arises due to individuals being in different stages at different times. Typically, couples experience Stages One and Two together, and then imbalances can occur as partners move through Stages Three, Four, and Five. Often couples get back in sync in Stage Six, as it requires them to work through and commit to the changes that have occurred or to break up. Knowing that it is normal for partners to be out of sync can be helpful. Acknowledging to your partner the stage you are in, what is going on for you, and what you need from each other during this time can reduce the dissonance that you may feel.

Sometimes the stages overlap. These stages aren't always cut-and-dry experiences. Couples may find that they move in and out of Stages Two and Three fluidly for many years. Other couples may have Stage Five moments and then shift quickly to Stage Six and back to Stages One through Three. Some couples may reside in Stage Four for years and then experience a significant challenge as Stage Five turns reality upside down, which is often the case with a midlife crisis. The most important thing to understand is that your relationship is an organic entity, constantly moving and adapting to the changes you are each making as individuals. Being aware of the life-cycle changes that can instigate stage shifts can help ease the transitions. Also, looking ahead and preparing for predictable upcoming changes, such as introducing children, empty nesting, and retirement, is advised.

Couples can get stuck. Many couples that eventually wake up in a dead relationship may find themselves stuck in Stage Six, "Us or Me." This happens when they commit to the status quo, or the third choice. This concept comes from Susan Jack, LMFT, an experienced couples therapist, who once shared with me that there are always three choices that a couple has in a relationship: (1) to stay, (2) to go, or (3) to maintain the status quo. When couples are unhappy *and* unwilling to move toward change, they remain clogged in the funnel of integration by choosing the status quo. This manifests into concrete patterns that can maintain discontent for years. Most of us have seen a relationship that has painfully continued year upon year, where the partners are content to complain about one another and never make any movement to change. Maybe you are experiencing that relationship. The only way out of this frozen state is to face your fears and stop resisting change. I encourage you to read on carefully and consider how you can move your relationship to a new place.

Couples merging families face multiple stages at once. Many couples step into subsequent love relationships that require bringing together two distinctly developed family systems. This can include children, ex-partners, stepparents, and larger extended family. This can be incredibly challenging and taxing on their new love relationship as the couple attempts to attach and bond, create a new stable "We," and navigate individual pursuits along with preexisting personal responsibilities. The added stress of managing other people's feelings about their relationship can take a toll on their feelings for each other. It can be helpful to realize that when these circumstances prevail, couples are often managing multiple stages immediately, even if their relationship isn't quite ready to take it all on. Extra understanding, patience, and grace for each other and the relationship are essential under these conditions.

This is not a perfect science, so there are exceptions along the way. It would be impossible to encapsulate every couple scenario and experience within this model. That is why there is always an exception to the rule. For the most part, couples often find themselves in these six stages; however, you may have a unique set of circumstances that sets your relationship apart. If that is the case, this model may illustrate the uniqueness of your relationship and what your distinct stages may be.

How Do the Stages Fit into the Lifespan of a Couple's Relationship?

Stage One—You and Me

The experience of falling in love doesn't often happen throughout our lifetime, yet we yearn for the incredible lovesick feeling and seek its replication. Throughout a couple's lifespan, they may find themselves "falling in love" with each other many times as they recommit and meet each other in a new way. This stage is found at the beginning of the relationship and is revisited when a couple moves through Stage Six and chooses the relationship all over again.

Important Lessons from Stage One

- *It feels* good *to be in love.* Remember to act like you did as lovers.

- *Little things matter.* Reach out and touch each other, send encouraging messages, and help each other out.

- *Focus on each other.* Pay attention to each other; really listen, care, and have empathy.

- *Be your* best *self.* Continue to make a positive impression on your partner; take care of your physical body and health. Pay attention to your mind, mood, and mental health.

Stage Two—We

The "We" couple is the foundation of couple and family life. This crucial stage happens initially when couples chose to commit to each other and the relationship. The first time a couple enters into Stage Two is critical because it writes the contract for the relationship going forward. Stage Two is also revisited following Stage Six as couples recommit and reestablish a new version of their relationship following seasons of change. These changes prompt a couple to review their original contract with each other, modify as necessary, and intentionally chose one another all over again.

Important Lessons from Stage Two

- *There's no "I" in team.* Remember, you are on the same team.

- *Without vision, couples perish.* Having shared goals brings purpose and energy that keeps couples together.

- *Stay engaged.* Doing the work of two all alone gets really lonely.

- *Be intentional.* This is *your* relationship. You are the one who needs to live in it and with it day after day. Make clear and thoughtful choices with your partner to make it the best it can be.

Stage Three—I and I

The timeline for Stage Three parallels Stage Two. As the relationship moves through the years and the "We" couple becomes established and reestablished, individuals will each foster their own development. Depending on the presence of children and how care for them is negotiated in the relationship, partners will continuously balance and rebalance opportunities for individual pursuits among family responsibilities. After children are raised, or if children are not a part of the couple relationship, other boundaries will define individual opportunities, such as money, time, career, and family obligations.

Important Lessons from Stage Three

- *Your partner won't meet all of your needs.* Your partner isn't perfect, superhuman, or a mind reader; you have to ask for what you need, and some needs you will have to fulfill on your own.

- *You are responsible for your happiness.* Feeling joy, contentment, satisfaction, and merriment in life starts *inside* of you.

- *Keep it interesting.* Continued individual growth and exploration can feed the relationship.

Stage Four—The We/I Plateau

The bulk of life is lived in the "We/I" Plateau as couples create and establish their own world together. This tends to be the resting place in the cycle where the relationship thrives yet can also suffer from the monotony of the day-to-day. If there was ever a time to be proactive in a relationship, it is during the "We/I" Plateau. Tending to your love life in the midst of the plateau will pay huge dividends in the future. Often, couples put relationships into cruise control during these years and wake up miles down the road, uncertain about each other. It doesn't have to be that way.

Important Lessons from Stage Four

- *There is always tension in balance.* Balance isn't a permanent state; it is a seesaw on which we are constantly in tension between self and others.

- *Sharing takes patience.* No matter how old you are, sharing things and taking turns can be hard.

- *Memories require time.* What is built in the everyday is often what is cherished for years to come.

- *Reach for alignment, and intentionally develop a vision for a shared future.* If you are working together toward the same goals, you have a better shot of coming out hand in hand.

Stage Five—The D-Factor

The D-Factor can be an unpredictable mystery. The why and when behind what triggers someone to ask fundamental, identity-critical questions is as unique to that individual as a snowflake is to the winter sky. However, there are some common times during the family life cycle that tend to instigate the D-Factor. These can include dealing with fertility issues, transitioning to new parenthood, launching children, experiencing an empty nest, the onset of retirement, reaching milestone birthdays, and suffering significant loss, death, or illness. These tend to be natural times of life reflection and reevaluation, which instigate questions about whom we are and whom we want to be.

Important Lessons from Stage Five

- *Everyone changes.* Remember that both you and your partner will face significant changes throughout your relationship; no one remains "the person I first fell in love with" forever.

- *Guard your heart.* Only you can "affair-proof" your marriage; your partner cannot control your individual choice to stay faithful to the commitment you have made. The D-Factor is a vulnerable time for other relationships to enter into the dyad. Talk with your partner about outside distractions before giving your heart to another relationship. An ounce of prevention here will save a pound of heartache.

• *Respect change.* Giving your partner space to discover himself or herself in the midst of your relationship is one of the highest forms of love. This is one of the "for better or for worse" moments you signed up for that will test your promise. Get support, work together, and trust the process.

Stage Six—Us or Me

Life-cycle changes that often instigate Stage Six are similar to Stage Five, again including fertility struggles, new parenthood, children leaving, the empty nest, and retirement. These are moments when couples often revisit their original contracts and commitments to one another. Other times may follow unanticipated changes such as the death of a child, family member, or close friend; a job change or move; financial gain or loss; health concerns, illness, or accidents; and/or divorces or crisis in other relationships close to the couple. All of these are occurrences throughout the life cycle that can lead a couple to question whether they should move on separately or begin a new season together in their relationship, effectively reentering the stages starting with Stage One.

Important Lessons from Stage Six

• *Rediscovery rocks.* Re-falling in love with your partner moves you to a deeper level of love not accessible before this time.

• *Time is an asset.* The time and energy you have put into a long-term, committed relationship is an asset. It is best to not take it for granted or sell it off too quickly.

- *Letting go can open new possibilities.* Releasing an old version of your relationship can bring much-needed new life to both partners, creating an updated version that brings great joy.

- *Endings can make room for new beginnings.* Sometimes ending the relationship, although painful, creates space for a fresh start.

- *Forgiveness is essential.* No matter what occurs in the relationship, your ability to forgive is an act that can bring great benefit to others and, more importantly, to yourself.

What Stage Is Your Relationship In?

Now it is your turn to take a look at the stages and assess where you, your partner, and your relationship fit. Only you know what stage or stages you and your partner may be in, if you and your partner are in the same place, and if there is any overlap occurring. You can define for yourself if what you are currently experiencing, problematic or otherwise, is normal for the relationship stage you are in. By understanding these stages, you will gain greater insight into yourself, your partner, and your relationship and have access to invaluable shared understanding, which will help strengthen your union. This allows you as a couple and as individuals to put your problems into perspective based on their relation to your current stage(s) of development.

Six-Stage Change Cycle for

Committed Couple Relationships Chart

STAGE	DEFINITION	LIFE-CYCLE CONNECTIONS	TIMELINE
One You and Me	ATTACHING	• Initial couple connection • Revisited following Stage Six	• Beginning of relationship • Following times of recommitment
Two We	ESTABLISHING	• Initial couple commitment • Revisited following Stage Six to renegotiate the couple contract	• Beginning of relationship • Following times of recommitment • Following changes in couple system
Three I and I	INDIVIDUATING	• Initial individual adjustment • Revisited throughout relationship as individuals pursue growth and development	• Beginning of relationship • Following changes in couple system • Following individual role changes
Four The We/I Plateau	STABILIZING	• Initial couple expansion • Revisited throughout relationship following adjustment to changes	• Beginning of relationship • Following adaptation to change
Five The D-Factor	DIFFERENTIATING	• Triggered by identity development events such as positive or negative change, loss, death, aging	• Anytime during or following Stage Two • Throughout the course of the relationship
Six Us or Me	INTEGRATING	• Following changes to the couple system • Following a D-Factor experience	• Following Stage Four or Stage Five • Brought on by couple challenges or invitation to change

{"Is This Normal?" Exercise}

CORE ELEMENT

Six-Stage Change Cycle of Committed Couple Relationships

Our relationship is in Stage ___6 (us)___.

My partner is in Stage ___5-6___.

I am in Stage ___6___.

(Your stages may all be the same or they may be different.)

These are some of the common experiences that we are facing: *[handwritten notes]*

These are some of the possible struggles for us: *[handwritten notes]*

Define a "normal" couple experience you thought was a unique problem for your relationship.

[handwritten notes]

How does working through the change cycle help shift your perspective about your relationship?

[handwritten notes]

3

Patterns–Drama to Durable

What if you could change just one thing in your relationship and feel a positive impact? Sounds like a miracle, right? Actually, it is possible if you know the right thing to change. Let's look at it this way. All relationships on the planet have one thing in common: They find a comfortable balance and commit to it. This balanced state is called homeostasis, simply defined as the process of maintaining equilibrium in a system. The world is full of systems that seek to maintain equilibrium. For example, human bodies find homeostasis to maintain a balance of optimum health. When the body falls out of homeostasis, guess what happens? It moves from a state of ease to becoming "dis-eased". In turn, we feel the symptoms that indicate the body is off balance. In response, our highly efficient physical body attempts to bring us back to health. For instance, when the immune system attacks a foreign invader in the body, we get a fever, which causes our body temperature to rise, and we experience shivers, chills, and aches. These symptoms indicate that the body is working to eradicate the presence of a virus or bacteria by making the environment unfavorable, all in an attempt to return the body to a normal, homeostatic state of functioning. Our bodies are smart, and when they are thrown off balance, the physical response to try to go back to health is immediate.

Nature operates in a similar fashion. Ecosystems find homeostasis through the necessary and delicate cycle of water distribution. Precipitation falls; rain and snow nourish the earth, bringing life to organisms, saturating the soil, filling watersheds, and supplying water to all living beings. Next, water is evaporated back into the air, returning to the atmosphere to repeat its purpose once again and ultimately creating a balanced water cycle. When water becomes scarce, such as during a drought, the whole ecosystem feels the impact. This change in the natural order affects the operation of the greater whole. Every part of an ecosystem must adapt to the change in water supply to find a new equilibrium.

Our couple relationships work in much the same way. As partners move into Stage Two and begin establishing their roles as a "We" couple, homeostasis occurs, securing the balance and bringing stability to the new relational system. This balance creates comfort for the couple throughout the relationship because it builds predictable interactions and dependable environments. Then, just like the body or an ecosystem when the balance of a couple's relationship is challenged through change, it responds with strong reactions to bring the couple back into balance or causes the couple to adapt to the changes creating a new homeostasis. Shifting one part of the system always affects the whole.

One of the guaranteed outcomes of homeostasis in a system is the development of patterns—organized and reliable ways of relating. In couple relationships, this is the way we learn to dance together, moving day in, day out, accomplishing the physical and emotional tasks that maintain our unity. Patterns are necessary to keep the balance of give-and-take as partners share life with one another. To avoid patterns altogether is to never bond into a working system, remaining two separate individuals who circle around each other without ever connecting. Initially, these patterns aren't very noticeable because they evolve naturally as partners meet each other's emotional and physical needs while building connection in the relationship. However, over the years, these balancing patterns can begin to feel monotonous and perhaps at times uncomfortable, even though they are needed to maintain the equilibrium.

As you read on, you will learn about the primary reasons homeostasis occurs and how, in response to these reasons, couples take on roles and create patterns that are unique to their relationship. You will then have the opportunity to assess the roles you play with each other and will be able to determine the patterns operating in your relationship. Also, we will look at how to shift roles and patterns to enhance the sustainability of your relationship. By understanding your roles and patterns and learning how to change even just one of them, you too can experience the positive impact mentioned at the beginning of this chapter.

Why Do Patterns Develop for Couples?

Functional Reasons for Patterns

Many patterns are created for purely functional purposes. They help us live and work together and establish a pace of life that brings stability and predictability. These types of patterns are created through delegation of tasks, and they help in the operation of our everyday lives. Sometimes they are intentionally decided upon and sometimes they emerge organically. Many of these patterns are established within the first committed year of being together, whether as a result of moving in together or getting married and living together for the first time. Functional patterns are typically developed by and attributed to the following elements:

Gender roles. In traditional relationships, gender roles may define the practical ways that we set up household tasks. In egalitarian relationships, shifting gender roles may help us determine who does what. Overall, gender roles often set functional patterns.

Skills. Who does it better? We often allocate tasks in relationships based on who has greater skill in a category. For example, one person is better with money, one is better at organizing, one is better at socializing, or one is better at remembering details. Whoever does it better takes on the job.

Passion. Who likes it more? In conjunction with skills is the element of passions. In each partnership, one partner is going to like certain tasks over others, and delegation naturally occurs through preference. Whoever likes it better takes on the job.

Tolerance. Tolerance relates to management of urgency. Partners often have differing levels of how soon something needs to get done. Typically, the one who experiences a higher level of urgency will take on the task. If they don't, the anxiety of managing their sense of urgency can lead to conflict. Over time, partners realize that taking on the task themselves reduces that stress.

Learned behavior. The families we grew up in have a significant influence on how we believe shared tasks are to be delegated. Sometimes partners find that they unconsciously take on a task or resist a task based on its compatibility with their observed upbringing. Couples can also experience conflict if they were modeled task delegation differently growing up, because they unconsciously assume it will be that way in their relationship.

Emotional Reasons for Patterns

Patterns also develop for emotional reasons, evolving as we negotiate our personal power and protect our vulnerability with one another. Often these patterns develop in healthy ways and create durability in the relationship, such as in mutual caring, where we each take turns supporting one another. Sometimes one partner is giving while the other is taking. Then they switch, sharing in being there for each other. Healthy emotional patterns exist when we can be honest, vulnerable, and persistent with each other about our feelings and experiences. However, that isn't always possible. When we are protecting how we feel, hesitant to address what we are experiencing, or unaware of our emotional needs, patterns can develop as coping mechanisms in our relationship. These are some of the issues that contribute to emotional patterns:

Conflict style. Each individual's personal tolerance for conflict and problem-solving can affect the patterns that develop. If couples are unaware of their differences, or are aware and haven't come to terms with how to manage their differences, a "typical" fight experience takes root. For example, if one person tolerates conflict well and likes to "talk things out," while the other become anxious with conflict and would prefer to avoid the situation, a pattern develops to help them manage their differing conflict styles. (More on this in the next chapter.)

Level of differentiation. As we discussed in the first chapter on relationship stages, differentiation is a lifelong development process. It also can affect patterns in relationships. When differentiation is low, there is a higher need for external approval. As differentiation increases, the need for external approval from others typically decreases. Patterns can occur to accommodate partners requiring less approval or more approval throughout the course of the relationship. Healthier patterns occur with an increased level of differentiation.

Attachment style. A partner's ability to connect and feel secure in the relationship is rooted in his or her personal attachment style. People can attach to one another in secure, insecure, or ambivalent ways based on how they were nurtured to connect in their early years of development and throughout previous intimate relationships. This plays a significant role in how couples organize their current relationship with one another. For example, if one partner feels secure and confident in the relationship but the other partner has insecurity about the commitment, patterns will emerge to maintain the imbalance of attachment in the system.

Learned behavior. How we behave in our adult intimate relationships is based on the intimate relationships we observed as children. It is amazing how many couples find their relationship patterns to be similar to what they saw in their parents' relationships. Although unsettling for many people, the impact of our family of origin is so embedded in the fabric of our being that it will continue to affect our current life if we are not conscious of it, and in turn, if we do not intentionally change our unwanted beliefs and behaviors.

Trauma history. For some partners, the lingering effects of an unresolved traumatic event or events in their history can cause an abreaction or overreaction in the present. An abreaction is when a partner's reaction to an issue in the present moment is overly exaggerated and seems much too big for the circumstances at hand because it is bringing forward the emotion of an unresolved past trauma. This experience can lead couples to build emotional patterns to manage the unresolved trauma(s). Sometimes this is conscious and couples know what they are protecting; other times this is unconscious, and the patterns develop over time without a clear understanding as to why they exist.

Understanding Relationship Patterns

As we have been learning, for both functional and emotional reasons, a variety of pattern configurations develop in all committed couples and are unique to every relationship. Patterns are predictable in that they require partners to take on "roles" in their interactions. If systems are maintained by patterns, patterns are maintained by roles. Roles are the characters we play with each other as we attempt to negotiate our power in completing tasks, caring for each other, and solving problems. In these roles, we dance together as the movements of one role induce a response from the other. These roles can be helpful and healthy, allowing people to dance well together, or they can be conflicting and challenging, causing the dance to become a power struggle.

There are two excellent lenses to look through that can help us understand the most common roles and patterns that exist in couple relationships. By utilizing the theories of the Drama Triangle and the Durable Triangle, we gain a complete picture of the couple dance. These theories illustrate how relationships are negotiated and were originally developed as a contribution to Eric Berne's psychological theory of transactional analysis (a fancy term for the study of relationships). The Drama Triangle was created by Stephen Karpman, MD in 1968 and was followed by the Durable Triangle by Lewis Quinby, LCSW. The great thing about the Drama and Durable Triangles are that they apply to so many aspects of relational life. They can be elevated to a macro level (think government and religion) or reduced to a micro level (think interpersonal and intrapersonal relationships) and the application still works. In all of my years studying relational models, I think these may be the most brilliant. I also believe that understanding our roles and their implications in relationships is life-changing information—the kind of information that, if you don't know it, has the power to leave you living at a deficit. What follows is an adaptation of the Drama and Durable theories as applied to couples to help you understand patterns and roles at work in your relationship.

What Are Roles?

Following are the primary roles that all couple patterns develop out of, creating either dramatic or durable functioning in a relationship. All couples and partners are susceptible to both Drama roles and Durable roles. I have never met anyone who hasn't played with all of these roles at one point or another. That said, shake off the part of you right now that wants to say, "I would never do that." It's OK; we all do it. Let's learn about the roles we all play.

Drama Roles

First, the Drama roles. These roles are positions used in our relationships that attempt to manage our influence over our partner and circumstances. We have been taught how to play these roles from the beginning of time, as they are primary in every great story. From fairy tales and epic adventures to television and movie plots, characters play these roles to maintain the drama in a story. We can also observe these same roles in larger systems like education, religion, and government as people work together to manage big organizations and address complex problems. Each of these Drama roles feed off each other in an attempt to solve a problem or complete a task while managing power in relationships. The trouble is that problems or tasks become complicated and difficult when using Drama roles because the process perpetuates drama through a power struggle rather than creating a peaceful resolution through reciprocity. Following is a definition of each Drama role:

The Buddy (AKA. Rescuer, Parent, Overfunctioning Partner)

The Buddy wants to fix everything in the relationship and make it all OK. The motivation to "fix" or "rescue" comes from the fact that doing so boosts the self-esteem of The Buddy. Without the job of fixing, who would The Buddy be? But all this help comes at a cost to both The Buddy and their relationship. Often The Buddy will "help" to the point of personal suffering, giving up valuable resources such as time, money, sleep, health, and work to save his or her partner. When the results of this suffering are felt, The Buddy feels like a martyr because what he or she gave up for their partner was "critical" to the cause of the relationship. There is a mentality that The Buddy is 100 percent responsible for what is happening for their partner and in the relationship. This does not allow The Buddy to share the joys or burdens with anyone, for it is his or her job to carry it all. Often, The Buddy will extend help without asking if the help is needed or wanted by their partner. This creates an environment of assumption and taking on unnecessary tasks, feeding into the feeling of being used and underappreciated. The Buddy also feels he or she is responsible for their partner's emotions because The Buddy has a hard time separating how he or she feels emotionally from how their partner feels. Overall, The Buddy takes on the role of a parent, managing their partner with the belief that he or she cannot do things for himself or herself. It is The Buddy's hope that caretaking in this manner will soothe his or her own uneasy emotions regarding what's going on in the relationship.

The Baby (AKA. Victim, Child, Underfunctioning Partner)

The Baby adopts a stance of being helpless or a victim in the relationship, the polar opposite of The Buddy. This attitude releases The Baby from responsibility as he or she assumes no ownership for what is going on. In doing so, The Baby takes little to no action in solving relationship problems. The Baby is not an active participant, but rather passive, letting life happen to him or her rather than engaging. Often when something needs to be addressed, The Baby will take a hands-off approach, avoiding the issue. The assumption is that someone else will take care of the problem. When challenged with why The Baby isn't helping or participating in the relationship, task, or problem, he or she responds with surprise and offers excuses, blames others, diverts the conversation and/or cries instead of talking. The Baby may communicate that he or she just isn't equipped to show up for various reasons beyond his or her control. Other times The Baby may make light of the situation, try to laugh it off, or minimize the reality to lighten the mood and attempt to push off concerns. Overall, The Baby takes on the role of a child, as an underfunctioning adult in the relationship, and makes it tough to move forward in a partnership.

The Bully (AKA. Persecutor, Bad Parent, Adolescent, Under or Overfunctioning Partner)

The Bully is the critic of the relationship and seeks to point out what is wrong and not working, ready for a fight and prepared to win. Often The Bully uses attacking actions and language that is demeaning, shaming, and blaming. When confronted by his or her partner, The Bully responds in defensive ways that might include self-righteous, "I told you so" attitudes. The Bully can also become the belligerent and stubborn adolescent, making life difficult through obstinate and uncooperative behavior. The Bully typically does not take responsibility to fix issues in the relationship, preferring to complain about his or her partner, the relationship, and the problem or task at hand. However, at times The Bully will take ownership if it validates his or her point or position. The Bully can range from using sarcasm and anger to ignoring and stonewalling in an effort to communicate feelings. Overall, The Bully takes on the power position of a bad parent by either overfunctioning and making their partner pay for it, or underfunctioning out of spite.

All three of the Drama roles operate with some commonality, helping to maintain the power in each position. Here are some similar elements that all Drama roles share:

- *Easily offended.* Each of these roles is emotionally reactive rather than responsive because they are not good at self-regulating; rather, they are regulated by external circumstance and the emotions of others.

- *Self-preserving.* The primary goal for each of these roles is to win or make sure their own personal interests are accomplished. This means they are motivated by what they think is going to get them what they want, not what is best for the relationship.

- *Quick to judgment.* Absorbed in their own points of view, there is no room for compassion and empathy for their partners. What may look like empathy is likely not authentic, as their ultimate goal is to take care of themselves first.

- *High use of complaining.* Using these roles perpetuates the problem rather than solving the problem, which leads to higher complaints or begging for change rather than pursuing change through individual adjustments. Partners would rather pass the blame than take ownership.

We all play each of these roles at one point or another in our relationships. To deny that is to deny we breathe. I am sure you can think of times in your relationship when you felt like you should fix things, when you felt like a victim, or when you felt self-righteous and critical. It is hard not to fall into these positions.

Each of us typically has a preferred role that is dictated by the role we played most frequently in our families growing up. What was the role you played in your family? Were you most often The Buddy, The Baby, or The Bully? That is the role that will feel most comfortable to you because you have the most experience playing it in life. You will use this role as a starting point when you enter into a Drama situation. What is important to know, however, is that none of these roles are static. You can start out as The Buddy, trying to fix everything, and then feel used and victimized and become The Baby, only to be justifiably irritated and emerge into The Bully. You will find that moving from role to role quickly can happen quite easily.

Couples can also swap roles effortlessly as they attempt to manage power issues in the relationship, trying one position that doesn't work and moving to another in hopes that it will help. This is nothing to be ashamed of. The truth is that as we process the myriad of emotions that exist in the complexity of couple interactions, we don't always present our best selves to one another. We manipulate our approaches in an attempt to find a resolution and conjure up assumptions to justify our choices. That is perfectly normal. Where the problem arises is in our unawareness. This is when our roles turn into fixed patterns that subject our relationship to the feeling that we are reliving the same drama over and over again.

Durable Roles

Fortunately, there are alternatives to the Drama roles, and most likely you and your partner are already using them in aspects of your relationship. These roles are Durable because they can be used over and over again without burning you out from fixing, making you feel like a victim, or turning you into a critic in your couple relationship. The primary difference between Drama and Durable roles exists in the management of power. Where Drama roles seek to take a power position, Durable roles strive to distribute power equally. When couples work together with durability, each partner participates with respect and reciprocity in addressing problems and completing tasks. All three of the following Durable roles can be exchanged for any of the Drama roles. Let's take a look at the Durable roles:

The Curious Collaborator

The Curious Collaborator looks at experiences and concerns in the relationship with reciprocity in mind. The Curious Collaborator wants to understand what is going on for himself or herself as much as what is going on with their partner. The Curious Collaborator understands that there are always two stories in a relationship and that hearing both is essential to progress. Responsibility is shared from this perspective; both partners own what is theirs and feel confident that each other will follow through. No one is picking up the slack unless it has been requested. Help is offered when it looks like it is needed, but if it is denied, that is OK too. The identity of The Curious Collaborator is secure whether their partner is happy or sad because The Curious Collaborator trusts that their partner can take care of himself or herself. However, The Curious Collaborator genuinely cares for their partner and is open to continued conversation about how he or she can be supportive.

The Authentic Ally

Utilizing assertiveness and honesty, The Authentic Ally seeks open dialogue. When The Authentic Ally senses a problem, he or she doesn't give up or run away but rather moves toward their partner and joins forces. Rather than separating from their partner and his or her problems, The Authentic Ally advocates for the relationship. The Authentic Ally is particularly useful in difficult situations because he or she strengthens the front of any battle by joining sides rather than fighting against others. The Authentic Ally realizes that working with their partner is an active choice; being passive isn't an option. The Authentic Ally owns his or her actions and any resulting consequences, and they are part of the solution instead of the problem. The Authentic Ally understands that problem-solving relies on transparency and openness.

The Persistent Partner

Knowing that real solutions require attention and patience, The Persistent Partner is in it for the long haul. Through well-defined boundaries, The Persistent Partner expresses what he or she needs and wants from their partner and the relationship. When The Persistent Partner feels angry, disappointed, or frustrated, he or she takes the time to process feelings and brings them to the relationship in a productive dialogue. The Persistent Partner understands the power of his or her words and can exercise restraint so as to not create bigger wounds. Through continuing dialogue, The Persistent Partner works on solutions. If their partner continues to disappoint or disrespect the relationship, The Persistent Partner is willing to follow through on consequences instead of just blowing empty threats. The ultimate desire is to make the relationship better, and The Persistent Partner will hang in there in pursuit of this goal.

Just like with Drama roles, there are common traits that all Durable roles share. Below are shared elements in the Durable roles:

- *Not easily offended.* Each of these roles is emotionally responsive rather than reactive. They are good at self-regulation and not controlled by external circumstances or the emotions of others.

- *Relationship preserving.* The primary goal for each of these roles is to make sure everyone's best interests are considered. Partners in these roles are motivated by win-win situations—they want to work together and protect each other.

- *Slow to judgment.* Partners who utilize these roles are notoriously open and curious and resist snap judgments. Assumptions are set aside, and concerns are discussed before coming to conclusions.

- *High use of respect.* These roles operate with the understanding that each partner is of great value and needs to be considered with honor. Partners treasure and want the best for each other, and each solution is focused on the greater good of the relationship.

Roles to Patterns

Now that we have reviewed the Drama roles and Durable roles that partners use in relationships, let's see how these roles come together to establish patterns. Earlier we touched on the concept of homeostasis, the inclination for a system to be balanced and predictable. We also looked at both functional and emotional reasons that patterns develop. For many reasons, couples find patterns quite naturally as they seek to achieve balance. Through using Drama roles, couples experience Drama patterns; likewise, through using Durable roles, couples experience the Durable pattern. Following are the patterns that develop and case examples to help you see how they play out in couple relationships.

As you read through the patterns, you will most likely see other people's relationships before you find your own. It is common that we can more readily identify for others what we cannot yet see in ourselves. Further, it may be clarifying to see your parents', sibling's, or friend's relationship. Once again, it normalizes the fact that all relationships use patterns. However, the actual value is to courageously observe how these patterns manifest in your relationship. Once you are aware, you can begin to understand their impact. And once you understand their impact, you can create effective change.

Drama Patterns

Operating in Drama patterns is quite common. But, as you will see, it wears on the couple's system and doesn't provide for a smooth, sustainable flow in the relationship. Just like the body can operate with a compromised immune system or an ecosystem can adapt during drought, the couple can live together in Drama patterns. However, each of the following scenarios has one thing in common: They don't wear well over time. When used year after year, they become like the childhood game of ring-around-the-rosy as couples dance around and around until they fall down, only to get up and do the same dance all over again. Exhausting! Let's take a look at the Drama patterns:

Drama Pattern One: The Buddy/Baby Pattern

The Buddy/Baby Pattern is quite common in committed couple relationships. It is an easy pattern to fall into as one person takes on the parent role and one partner the child. Sometimes this pattern is isolated to specific areas of a relationship, like financial management or household duties. But often it becomes the climate of the relationship, where one person takes on the role of being responsible (overfunctioning) and the other goes along for the ride (underfunctioning). Due to this climate, it isn't uncommon for problems to arise in a couple's sex life from the unattractive, disjointed power balance. Although typically functional in the early years, the Buddy/Baby Pattern can eventually beget bitterness and resentment later on.

What the Buddy/Baby Pattern Can Look Like: The Midlife Meltdown

Scott and Mary had been married for eighteen years, lived an upper-middle-class lifestyle, and had three kids and one dog. Scott came to therapy first, although it wasn't the first time he had been to see a couples therapist. Together they had seen someone in years three and eight of their marriage. Mary had led the visits early on and those sessions, although enlightening, hadn't produced any real, sustainable change. This time around was different. Scott was convinced, although Mary adamantly denied it, that Mary was having an affair with a mutual friend, Dave. He was devastated and confused by what he had done wrong. He had provided an incredible life, from a beautiful home to amazing vacations. They had smart, talented kids. Frankly, it was a life to be envied by most, so what in the world was wrong?

Shortly after, Mary joined the therapy sessions. She appeared indifferent and exhausted, explaining that she had spent years begging Scott to pay attention. It was common that she would take care of everything around the house while also reminding him of appointments, important dates, and events, to pick things up, to put things away, and even to call her and bring her flowers. After so many years of nagging, their sex life had become stale; they made love infrequently, primarily because she just didn't desire him the way she used to. Mary had checked out, and Scott was defensive. He felt that he had provided a great life, they had built wonderful memories, and as far as he could see, although the nagging was a pain in the butt, their time together was a pretty "normal" marriage. Sure, he didn't always remember stuff, but was it really that bad?

In this case, Mary took on the role of The Buddy, overfunctioning and, in turn, often "parenting" her partner's life. This made her feel useful, in control, and often like a martyr. Scott was playing the role of The Baby by deferring responsibility and minimizing Mary's concerns. He did not want to see himself as a child but realized he frequently deferred responsibility to Mary, not sure how to be helpful at times.

The Buddy/Baby Pattern often appears like a "pretty normal 'relationship'". As a matter of fact, it is a typical portrayal of most TV families—an overresponsible wife and a childlike husband (even if he is able to keep an excellent job with a significant income). Unfortunately, this is not the making of a long-term, highly satisfying relationship. It takes its toll when both partners don't show up with a reciprocal interest in the day-to-day responsibilities of family and life. Both Scott and Mary had to see how their roles were maintaining the pattern. Neither one was all right or all wrong. Mary had to stop overfunctioning for Scott and allow him to try to show up or face the consequences of his lack of action. This wasn't easy for her. Scott had to start writing things down and paying attention to details. If he needed help, he had to ask for it rather than just assuming things would be taken care of. This wasn't easy for him. Slowly, over time they started to experience a new balance and came to appreciate one another in a new way. This increased their respect for each other and opened the door for intimacy to resurface.

Drama Pattern Two: The Buddy/Bully Pattern

The Buddy/Bully Pattern operates as a parent/adolescent relationship. One partner overcompensates for the other partner's difficult or adolescent behavior. This relationship takes on an enabling effect as The Buddy often justifies and accommodates for the Bully's negative and critical reactions. This can occur through performing physical tasks in an attempt to pacify and please The Bully, as well as emotional management of other people and circumstances, in an effort to keep The Bully from reacting. There tends to be a "walking on eggshells feeling" for The Buddy, which limits intimacy and maintains an emotional distance in the partnership. The Bully is often demanding and unaware of how their attitude and behavior is affecting those around them, while The Buddy is hyperaware to the point of orchestrating interactions to prevent negative experiences for everyone involved.

What the Buddy/Bully Pattern Can Look Like:

The Uneven Team

Alex and Stephen had been together for twenty years. They met in their late twenties at a business conference for young executives. The connection was immediate. They both said they felt comfortable and at home with each other right away. After dating for a few years long distance, they settled in the same city and shortly after celebrated their commitment with family and friends. After that, they considered having children, but their careers were time consuming, and they felt the window just eventually closed. When they began to discuss their relationship, Stephen was quite reserved and logical, while Alex was very demonstrative, the kind of person that energizes a room when they walk in the door. It seemed a classic case of opposites attract.

They both felt the difference in their personalities was positive in their relationship, although at times it did cause problems. Alex depended on Stephen's leadership and emotional steadiness, while Stephen credited Alex for their exciting and vibrant social circle.

The trouble was that, all too often, Stephen was mopping up Alex's messes. This had been an ongoing issue from the beginning of their relationship, including financial irresponsibility, a series of job losses, and embarrassing behavior out in public. These experiences typically created feelings of frustration for Stephen, but he put up with it because, as he understood, that was just a part of loving Alex. Also, for as many times as he begged for change, nothing ever shifted. On the other hand, when these circumstances occurred, Alex responded defensively, blaming others for his bad behavior, and struggled to accept any constructive criticism. He would often lash back with an adult version of a temper-tantrum that was overwhelming for those around him. At this point in their relationship, Stephen was tired and wasn't sure he wanted any more drama. Alex was devastated and was finally willing to consider owning part of the problem.

At first glance, the Buddy/Bully Pattern often appears to be solely the fault of The Bully and, truth be told, the Bully position can be very difficult to modify without the partner in this position acknowledging their contribution to the problem. One of the sustaining aspects of this pattern is The Buddy taking full responsibility and The Bully taking none. However, it takes both The Buddy and The Bully to keep the pattern entrenched. The Buddy, acting as an enabler, continues to allow The Bully's behavior by taking on a parental role and treating The Bully like a bad child who needs a handler, rather than an adult who needs to be accountable. The Bully depends on this setup to continue damaging, irresponsible actions.

In this case, Stephen needed to learn that as long as he continued to manage Alex's consequences, he was contributing to the drama. Also, Alex needed to be challenged to own the negative results of his choices before looking to Stephen to solve the problem. The adjustments of both partners were critical for them to start to find a new balance in the relationship. The Buddy/Bully pattern can be one of the hardest to change, as both partners need to create and accept new boundaries in the relationship. For Stephen and Alex, it took a long time, with support, for each of them to see the other as an equal partner. However, the outcome allowed them to maintain a long-term relationship that they both deeply desired.

Drama Pattern Three: The Bully/Baby Pattern

The Bully/Baby experience feels like a bad parent-child relationship where one partner dominates while the other submits. This power dynamic is typically maintained through a combination of criticism and passivity. The Bully will often over-function with help that is conditional and delivered with an undermining attitude; in response, The Baby under-functions, acting helpless and lacking assertiveness. The Bully continually discards compassion and empathy and instead uses the relationship to validate his or her need to be better, right, and in control. The Baby remains weak and needy in hopes that his or her partner will eventually notice their victim state and change or save him or her.

What the Bully/Baby Pattern Can Look Like:

The Missed Moments

Kevin and Leah had been together for five years. They didn't have any children yet but were hoping to start a family in the next couple of years. However, before they actually started trying, they thought they needed to work on the fighting in their relationship. The weekend before they came to therapy, they had what they referred to as "one of those fights". As they relayed the story of the weekend, Leah's lip trembled, her hands shook, and tears filled the rims of her eyes. Kevin, on the other hand, was bright red and looking down at his feet. Leah proceeded to share that sometimes Kevin got so mad about the littlest things and then said such mean things to her. Afterward, she continued, he always said he was kidding and laughed it off. And sometimes, when they were out with other couples, he made fun of her in front of them and revealed personal things that were embarrassing to her. Instead of criticizing him too or justifying his behavior, Leah explained that she got silent and didn't talk to him the rest of the night.

Kevin didn't disagree with Leah's story. However, he added that whenever he had a complaint about the relationship and brought it up to Leah, she started crying, shut him out, and wouldn't tell him what was wrong. This frustrated Kevin. He grew up in a family of all boys where there was lots of kidding around and giving each other a hard time. It never meant anything. Leah grew up as an only child and spent a lot of time around adults; she was well taken care of and spoken to respectfully. Kevin's way of communicating was tough for her to understand. Both of them felt like having kids was only going to make this worse and wondered if there was something they could do to make it better. They did acknowledge that there were times when they really enjoyed each other's company and supported each other emotionally. But, after five years of these moments, the hurts were piling up and not getting resolved. Kevin came to understand that he had adopted the role that was familiar to him from his childhood—The Bully. As a matter of fact, it felt so normal to him that he didn't even realize the damage it was causing the relationship. Leah, on the other hand, was so used to being emotionally coddled that she fell quickly into The Baby role. She needed to find her voice and assert herself with Kevin to be heard.

As you can see, the Bully/Baby Pattern can be fairly destructive, and in some couple's interactions it can border on being abusive. The continual experience of one partner criticizing while the other passively responds builds layers of wounds in the relationship that eventually create an emotional brick wall that is hard to break down. Often these roles were learned well in each partner's childhood, whether through parental modeling or sibling dynamics. This, in turn, makes couples initially unaware of the long-term damage it can do to their relationship.

Both Leah and Kevin needed to make some changes if they wanted the relationship to get back to a safe place. Leah needed to toughen up a bit and become more assertive. When she felt like responding through tears, she needed to tell Kevin she needed a minute to process what he was saying. Even then, when she engaged in the conversation and had tears, she also had to use her words. Kevin needed to realize that what maybe wasn't a "big deal" to him was to his partner. If she told him it was too much, that was his cue to back down and apologize. They developed a code word for when they were out with others so Kevin would know if he crossed a line. None of these modifications were easy, but they were the key to this couple shifting their Drama pattern with one another.

Drama Pattern Four: The Buddy/Buddy Pattern

The Buddy/Buddy Pattern plays off the need to be caretakers. In this dynamic, both partners are fixers and feel overly responsible for the relationship and each other. Often they will be trying to save or help each other to sustain the illusion of being in control, which protects their emotions. Underneath this behavior is the belief that

"I am essential to others succeeding in the world." But in this case, both partners feel that way about each other and the world they live in together. The overfunctioning of both partners creates an atmosphere of limited intimacy and vulnerability between partners because it is difficult to let your guard down when you are in charge. The need to be responsible and take care of things creates a buffer and, in turn, emotional distance. To let go and have others take care of you means to be out of control and dependent, which is not in the nature of this role. Beyond overfunctioning in the relationship with each other, this couple often also helps others at the expense of the couple relationship and family life.

What the Buddy/Buddy Pattern Can Look Like:
The Crazy Caretakers

Laurie and Shannon had been together for six years and shared the parenting of three children, all from Shannon's previous relationship. They came in for couples therapy because, as much as they cared about each other, their relationship was feeling more and more like a friendship rather than a romantic connection. When they talked about their life with each other, they conveyed that they were the go-to couple in the neighborhood. If anyone needed help, they were always up for the task. Whether it was planning a block party, taking care of the neighbor's kiddos, or pet sitting, they would always say yes. Over the years, they had both learned that the best way to get people to like them was to give, and often they did that to their own detriment. As a result, they would end up fighting, sometimes from being overcommitted and not having time for what they really wanted to do, and other times over money because Laurie was so giving she would spend beyond the agreed-upon budget. After these fights, Shannon would feel sorry and pick up a few more hours at work to make up for the deficit; after all, Laurie was just trying to be helpful. It was also common that Shannon would take the kids on unplanned weekends to help out her ex at the last minute. Even though Laurie rarely complained about this, she was harboring a lot of hurt feelings over broken plans and time lost for the two of them. Both Laurie and Shannon were deeply entrenched in playing The Buddy role. Each of them used the power associated with giving as protection from people's disapproval and to create acceptance. For personal reasons, they had both come to the same conclusion—being in control is safer.

As the Buddy/Buddy pattern continues, there is a perceived sense of intimacy because couples believe they are doing the "right things," the giving feels good, and there are so many justifiable reasons for sacrificing. However, these couples are usually giving away the pieces of their relationship that create stability and intimate connection with each other. They often justify and minimize hurt feelings, allowing them to accumulate and become a barrier to intimacy over time.

For Laurie and Shannon to break this pattern, they both needed to learn the value of the word *no*. Because it wasn't in their nature to set boundaries that benefited themselves and the relationship, there was quite a learning curve as they started to keep their time together sacred. They were drawn to the airplane oxygen metaphor. You know the drill that flight attendants go through before a plane takes off? They review the exits, the seat belts, and the floatation devices and then tell you, "In the case of the loss of oxygen, a yellow bag will drop out of the ceiling. If you are traveling with small children, please put the bag on yourself first and then on your child." This sounds so counterintuitive, but if the parent is passed out from lack of oxygen, no one is available to help the child. This was fitting in Laurie and Shannon's relationship, and as they pursued better boundaries, they would remind one another that if they didn't first put the oxygen on their relationship, they wouldn't be any good at helping anyone else. They also needed to take turns receiving from each other, not just being in the position of giving. Practicing this allowed them to increase their vulnerability and connection, building successful intimacy habits that helped bring back romantic feelings and benefited the relationship long term.

Drama Pattern Five: The Bully/Bully Pattern

A hallmark of the Bully/Bully Pattern is the constant nitpicking, or back-and-forth criticism, that is reminiscent of two siblings in the backseat of a car on a long road trip. These partners consistently approach each other negatively, which creates an environment where both partners feel defensive, and in turn, justified by the need to be right. They often relate through sarcasm and demeaning language. They may complain about each other, causing conflict in the relationship, or they may bond by complaining about and criticizing others. This couple rarely lets their guard down with each other, and when they do, it is usually quickly remedied by a snarky put-down, returning them to their comfortable critic pattern.

What the Bully/Bully Pattern Can Look Like:
The Culture Clash

Raquel and Tim had been together for nine years and had a four-year-old son. They came from dramatically different cultural backgrounds. Her family had never accepted him as the "right" choice for their daughter and had been very open with letting Tim know what they thought. This created loyalty issues for Raquel as she straddled the tension between her family and her partner. As a couple, they spent most of the time at odds with each other but occasionally got on the same page when it felt like them against the world. They recalled that some of their most bonding conversations would occur on the ride home from her parents' house after a holiday dinner. They would both complain about how awful her family treated Tim and how they would never put their child in that position. But most of the time, their frustrations were aimed at each other. From big differences to the little things, they just would not let each other off the hook. Over time they came to discover that blaming each other for their differences and problems was destroying their relationship.

By the time they entered into therapy, the only positive thing they could agree on was their child. They both desired to be good parents and felt proud of their son. Both Raquel and Tim felt the rest of their life together was riddled with irreconcilable differences. As they each took a long, hard look at their negative attitudes, they had a collective aha moment. Throughout her childhood, Raquel had learned that being different, although lonely at times, was what made her unique and special. It gave her power. Tim had a similar experience. He grew up very intellectual and built an identity on his quick mind and being the smartest guy in the room. This made him feel powerful. They both learned to feel important and in control by being separate from others. In turn, they both maintained power in their relationship by staying at odds with each other. This realization actually brought them closer together and increased empathy in their relationship.

Unfortunately, the Bully/Bully Pattern can become a way of life. Couples don't even realize how critical they have become. Complaining is addictive; it creates a charged, negative energy, and when that isn't present, partners can get bored and uncomfortable. Couples with this pattern may go through withdrawal as they work to shift the energy from negative to positive in their environment. Also, learning to be powerful without being critical can be tough. After Tim and Raquel's aha moment, they started to work on softening with one another. By reducing their defensive reactions and increasing compliments and praise, their relationship took a turn for the better.

Drama Pattern Six: The Baby/Baby Pattern

When the Baby/Baby Pattern occurs, couples find themselves in a helpless relationship. Not much gets accomplished when both partners commit to a victim mindset. There can be plenty of conversation about what needs to be done, but each partner has justifications for why it is not his or her responsibility for making it happen. Both partners are underfunctioning and don't feel the need or urgency to fix or take responsibility for what isn't working in the relationship or in their life together. They get stuck in complaining and blaming, looking continually outside of their individual contribution to find external reasons for their dissatisfaction and discontentment. This can include blaming their partner, other relationships, and physical or environmental experiences for their continual unhappiness and lack of success, putting positive change outside of their control.

What the Baby/Baby Pattern Can Look Like:

The Un-Dreamers

Steve and Kim spent the first three years together living in Steve's mom's house. At that time, Kim was in school, and Steve didn't make enough money at his job for them to afford a very nice place to live. When they finally did move out, it was because Steve's mom remarried and her new husband moved into the house. Kim came to therapy first because she was feeling really depressed. She had graduated from school and was having a hard time finding a job. She was bright and had acquired a good degree, but she didn't think very highly of herself and often wouldn't follow through after an interview. It had been almost a year of looking for work, and she was really discouraged. She also wasn't feeling great about her relationship with Steve because she felt she was the most motivated of the two, which wasn't saying much. Steve eventually joined us and echoed Kim's feelings but said he just figured that was what long-term relationships were like—you get into a rut and wait it out.

Over time, Kim and Steve came to understand that they both had shared dreams but really didn't know what to do to make them happen. Step by step, they started to see some progress. Kim finally got a job, and the extra money helped pay off some debt. With the new financial freedom, Steve became energized around fixing up their new place, increasing their pride in their home and belief that they could move forward. Together, they learned how to stop waiting for the other one to make something happen first and that to achieve their dreams, each of them needed to contribute.

Often The Baby/Baby Pattern creates a sense of apathy and is born out of circumstances that can feel victimizing. Other times it can come about because of low self-worth, reduced expectations from life, coming from a family system that had overfunctioning parents that took care of everything for the children, or a history of actually being victimized. Moving out of this pattern requires a shift in thinking and changing long-held beliefs. Both Kim and Steve were able to achieve a new level of self-efficacy by associating their actions with personal accomplishments. As they did this individually, they were able to encourage each other and express how proud they were of each other. This created a momentum that carried over into what they believed they could do together.

Drama Pattern Seven: The Drama Dance Pattern

Because patterns are predictable, most couples will experience each other in specific, dedicated roles the majority of the time. This is what sustains the homeostasis in the relationship. However, at times couples will also find that they dance through all of the roles as they attempt to process a problem in the relationship. Following is an example of what it looks like as couples change positions and do the Drama Dance Pattern.

What the Drama Dance Pattern Can Look Like:
The Secret Debt

Chip and Shelly had been married for five years when they came to couples therapy. They had met through mutual friends and were initially amazed to find out how similar their lives were. Shelly, a nurse, was a caregiver by nature. Chip, a teacher, was filled with passion for learning. These are both professions that their parents held, so they equally understood the value of what each other did for a living. After two great years dating, they were excited to finally get married and build a life together. Unfortunately, within the first year of their marriage, the relationship started to unravel.

By the time they came into therapy, they were stuck in a Drama Dance that was already getting old. They explained the following scenario: Shortly after the honeymoon, Shelly found out that Chip had some massive debts he had never told her about. His dishonesty hurt her and made her angry, but she, being the caretaker at heart, became The Buddy and worked overtime to help him pay the debt. This required late nights and long shifts, which brought out the martyr in her. When she would complain to Chip that she was exhausted and didn't think there was any way she could keep up the double shifts, he would listen but took no action to help pay the bills. Often she would come home late from work to find him sitting on the couch, dishes in the sink, playing The Baby by complaining about how tired he was from teaching all day. This comment would then shift Shelly into The Baby role also, feeling like a victim, taken advantage of by

Chip and helpless to move him to action. After all, if he had only been honest and responsible at the beginning of their relationship, they wouldn't be in this situation. Shelly would express this to Chip, who would then become defensive and frustrated, turning into The Bully. He would start blaming her for overworking, saying that if she was tired it was her fault because he never asked her to solve his problem. Terribly wounded from his lack of sensitivity and gratitude, Shelly would go to bed confirmed in her victim status. Many of these nights, Chip would just sleep on the couch.

In the morning, Shelly would wake up mulling over the previous night's interaction, and by the time she reached the kitchen, she was ready to let Chip have it. In full Bully mode, Shelly would start to shame him, telling him a real man would take action and not let his wife work overtime. After a long monologue, Chip would be in tears, proclaiming his love for Shelly, apologizing and committing to getting a second job by the end of the week. Unfortunately, there was always a justified reason Chip didn't get a second job, and Shelly continued to put in for extra shifts to make the debt payments. This Drama Dance Pattern had been going on for over four years and had contributed to many other disconnections in their relationship, including little to no time spent together and a dried-up sex life. They were on the verge of ending the relationship.

The Drama Dance Pattern is easy to swing through as partners trigger each other to move from role to role. There is an illusion that the problem is being solved, but, in the end, nothing changes. For Chip and Shelly, it was only after they both realized the game they were in together and the roles they were playing that they were able to start to change their circumstances. By the time they finished with therapy, they had paid off the debts, returned to normal work schedules to allow time for one another, reestablished an intimate sexual connection, and, most importantly, had forgiven each other for the years of pain. They also learned that playing Drama roles in their relationship with each other wasn't how they wanted to continue in the future. Through observing their roles and shifting their behavior, the pattern started to change.

Drama Pattern Maintenance

The couples in the above scenarios were all reacting to the challenging and uncomfortable issues that occur in every relationship. However, it wasn't just their reactions that kept the drama going. So, what keeps Drama patterns sustained in a couple's relationship? Typically, Drama patterns are maintained for one of the following three reasons:

1.   The issue at hand is something that the couple doesn't want to address. It is easier to dance around it and hope it will change than to call it out directly.

2.   The issue has been addressed without any positive and/or sustainable change. This creates an environment of insanity, doing the same things over and over again but expecting different results.

3.   There is important information about the issue that is still unknown to the couple. The couple, in the dark about what is really going on, stays in a reactive state with each other, believing issues will eventually get better or resigning to live in drama.

Getting stuck in undesirable Drama patterns, for both functional and emotional reasons, is common. Patterns get comfortable and keep the relationship going even if we don't like them or they make us feel crazy. This is where my original stance about changing one thing and finding a positive impact comes into play. It is important to know that you can change the patterns that aren't working in your relationship. As you change your role in a pattern, it automatically invites your partner to change how he or she reacts. Just like Chip and Shelly, once you understand the roles and patterns in your relationship and start to notice when they are present, you can work to change them by shifting your role from Drama to Durable. Notice that I didn't say by shifting your partner's role. Rather, *you* shifting *your* role becomes the change agent in the relationship, pressing to create a new homeostasis. Let's take a look at what you can do.

Durable Pattern

The key to moving from Drama to Durable is as easy as exchanging a Drama role for a Durable role. OK, I know this is easier said than done, but I also know that you *can* do it! When couples move into Durable roles, they create a sustainable relationship pattern that utilizes respect, vulnerability, and reciprocity. No longer are partners trying to manipulate the other person to resolve their own emotional discomfort. Nor are they attempting to protect and manage their personal power at the expense of their partner. Rather, durability is a very clear and flexible way to relate, which is why it creates only one pattern. Following is an example of a couple that worked through a problem in their relationship with durability.

What the Durable Pattern Can Look Like: Growing Pains

Sarah and Tom initially met in a big city where they both were pursuing careers that they enjoyed. They recollected their dating life with a smile and described those years as "the best time of our life." Eventually, they married and were thrilled when they found out they were expecting a baby girl. At that point, they decided to move back to a smaller city closer to their families. They came in for couples therapy after making this transition. At this point, their daughter was almost two years old, and they were in the thick of it. Tom had reestablished himself in a fast-paced firm that had demanding hours and a bar that was always moving higher. Sarah was attempting to rebuild her career around caring for their daughter and was not feeling like she was doing either very well. They had little time for each other, and Tom's health was taking a hit from the high stress.

This was a very easy scenario for the Drama patterns to rule, but this couple seemed to do things differently. Although Sarah was tempted to fix things for Tom at times, she knew that only Tom could help himself. She offered to support him by reducing his responsibility around the house while also authentically sharing the toll his unmanaged stress was putting on her and the relationship. She missed him. She was tired of his late hours and the fact that he was constantly on his phone and distracted when he came home. She told him she was lonely and their current lack of intimacy made her feel unwanted and unattractive. Tom took this all in, and instead of getting defensive or putting the blame elsewhere, he told Sarah that he missed her too. He felt stuck and anxious. He felt he was failing as a husband and a dad. He feared that she didn't have enough time to pursue her career, which he knew made her happy. Together they became Authentic Allies.

Next, Tom and Sarah moved into the role of Curious Collaborators as they brainstormed what kind of actions they could each take to positively affect the relationship. They then instigated those changes. Tom saw a doctor and pursued a path to better health. Sarah hired childcare and spent more dedicated time working. Together they created boundaries between time spent focused on work and time spent as a family; this included a phone curfew in the evening where they shut off outside distractions. Finally, they made arrangements for a weekend away and were so excited to report that they had reconnected in ways they hadn't for years.

Slowly they both started to feel better. Some days were easier than others. On the hard days, the Persistent Partner role would engage as they reminded each other to slow down, try again, and not give up. Through this tough time, they each took ownership of their individual experiences and needs while together pursuing their relationship and family life. Ultimately, by resisting the drama roles of The Buddy, The Baby, and The Bully, a Durable pattern became their way of living, building the foundation for a relationship that could be sustained through good times and challenging transitions.

Moving from Drama to Durable

Patterns in their purest form are not right or wrong; rather, they are the unavoidable result of a balanced system. As you learned about the functional and emotional reasons for patterns, the Drama and Durable roles, and the common relationship patterns that emerge, you may be tempted to judge their value. Instead, try to critically examine whether your active patterns are helping or hurting your relationship. This approach is a much better motivation for change. As you now know, some patterns are necessary and even facilitate getting things accomplished. Other patterns, even if comfortable, may be helping you to avoid issues you don't want to deal with or change. Only you can assess if this is happening in your relationship.

Identify what you are doing to maintain unwanted Drama patterns and choose to move into a Durable pattern. Maybe you are always picking up after your partner's messes, like a Buddy, and instead, you become a Curious Collaborator, wondering what things would be like if you stopped caretaking your partner. Let go of your need to fix the problem, tell your partner what you can do and what you cannot do for them, and then see what happens. Maybe when you don't get your way, you act like a Bully, becoming critical and defensive, pushing your partner away. Next time, talk respectfully and listen even if it is hard, and take on the attributes of a Persistent Partner. Let your partner know that you are making a change, and even if it is difficult, you are not going to be a Bully anymore. Maybe you feel like your partner doesn't consider your feelings, leading you to feel victimized and like a Baby. Instead become an Authentic Ally, take ownership of how you feel and what you need, and then tell your partner openly instead of shutting down and waiting for him or her to figure it out or ask you what is wrong.

There are so many ways that you can change. Every interaction with your partner is a new opportunity to pursue a Durable pattern. Here are some suggestions on how to move into Durability:

If You're a Buddy Try Becoming a Curious Collaborator

- Own your part of a problem, and change what you can. Talk with your partner about what he or she can also do, so you are working on the problem together.

- Offer help in ways you are able, not in ways that will create suffering. Give what you can and don't burn yourself out—you aren't any good in the relationship that way.

- If your partner doesn't want help, accept his or her "No." Learn to support, not fix, your partner.

- Be confident in who you are in your relationship, and respect your partner as a responsible grown-up.

If You're a Baby Try Becoming an Authentic Ally

• Realize that as an adult, you aren't helpless, and you have choices to change your circumstances.

• Choose the efficient path of authenticity and honesty rather than shutting down. Use your voice, and ask for what you need or want.

• Choose to own your actions and consequences. Again, as an adult, you are not a victim in your own world.

• Discuss your feelings even in stressful situations. Nothing will change if you stay silent.

• Actively seek solutions when there is a problem rather than waiting around for your partner to fix things.

If You're a Bully Try Becoming a Persistent Partner

• Communicate clearly, and don't expect your partner to be a mind reader.

• Have a respectful conversation even when you're disappointed.

• Don't react and beat your partner up through your words and actions.

• Take time to understand your anger and express it productively. If you can't speak it, write it.

• Don't manipulate your partner or operate in self-serving ways; relationships are a team sport.

• Be aware that there can be more than one perspective; try to determine what your partner thinks before jumping to conclusions.

What Are Your Relationship Patterns?

Changing established patterns can seem overwhelming at first, but shifting your role is the one thing you can do that can have an immediate impact. Once you start using a new Durable role the pattern in your relationship has to respond. Remember, relationships are complex systems like the human body or an ecosystem. Patterns are established to create predictable function and secure stability. When something new is introduced or something familiar is removed, the system needs to adapt to the change and integrate into a new functioning pattern. It may not be comfortable at first.

As we have discussed in depth, change is not easy in a relationship. But once a change is initiated, it is only a matter of time for the relationship to adapt to a new balance of comfort. Here's a helpful tip: Patterns are easier to adjust when *both* partners can agree on what needs to be modified and are *both* willing to work on shifting their roles. Together, choose one pattern that isn't working well in your relationship, and then decide how you can start to make useful changes. The following exercise will help you out.

{"Is This Normal?" Exercise}

CORE ELEMENT
Predictable Patterns in Committed
Couple Relationships

What are some functional reasons for patterns in your relationship? *PC or scale*

What are some emotional reasons for patterns in your relationship? *N Clur*

My common Drama role is _____.

My Partner's common Drama role is _____.

Our most common Drama pattern is _____.

These are some of the typical experiences that we are facing because of our Drama pattern:

— N/A

These are some reasons we may want to change our Drama pattern: *N/A*

How could I shift my Drama role to a Durable role in order to change our pattern? *N/A*

4

Styles–All Couples Fight

All couples have conflicts; some are immediately solvable, and some will go the distance in the relationship. Much research has been done on couple conflict, and one of the fascinating outcomes is the fact that all couples have chronic conflicts that remain throughout the length of their relationship. This means that it is perfectly normal to be in a relationship with unsolvable problems and disagreements. Are you breathing a sigh of relief? So often couples believe that the presence of conflicts, particularly unsolvable ones, means that there is a fundamental problem with the overall relationship. Couples may think, "We are just not the right match," when the truth is that you are going to find sustainable conflict in any relationship you have with anyone. Really, at the end of the day, it is what you believe about conflict that is going to cause you the most discomfort. If you see conflict as threatening, then any presence in your relationship will be bad; if you see conflict as just a difference of opinion or different ways of seeing the world, then it can be much more manageable. This sounds easy, but along with conflict comes anger, and anger is a complex emotion for most people to manage.

The Dr. Johns

We all work with emotion differently. How you experience anger will be different from how your partner experiences anger, just like how you experience happiness will be different from how your partner experiences happiness. This is because you have each been bathed in a unique emotional bathtub. Who you each grew up with in your family system drew the bath for your definitions of emotion as you lived with them day after day, absorbing their emotional expressions. How anger or happiness was expressed in your family environment verbally and nonverbally through your parents and caregivers sets a baseline for how each of you will define what these (and other) emotions look and feel like for you personally.

This process is called *learned affect*. Dr. John Omaha's study of emotions defines learned affect as the foundational education of what we understand emotion to look and feel like. Dr. Omaha explains that how emotions are communicated by the family we grow up in is how we learn to define and express those emotions later in life. So if you grow up in a family where anger is big and loud, you absorb that emotional experience, and that is how anger is defined for you. If you grow up in a family where anger is quiet and subdued, you absorb that emotional experience and that is how anger is defined for you. By looking at it this way, can you imagine how many different ways anger can be defined? The chance that you and your partner were raised with the exact same definition of anger is highly unlikely. And this unavoidable difference contributes to one of the primary difficulties when it comes to conflict: We often don't experience anger in the same way.

You see, anger is a catchall emotion that can be best explained as an iceberg experience. Like an iceberg, anger is the top emotion sticking out of the water, resulting from reactions to a variety of other negative feelings found underneath it, such as disappointment, hurt, fear, confusion, and frustration. When faced with people, ideas, or experiences that are in opposition to how we like our world to work, these negative feelings can surface as anger. In turn, how you have learned to manage these negative emotions during disagreements develops your individual conflict style.

The other Dr. John is one of the foremost researchers on couple relationships. Dr. John Gottman has been observing how couples navigate their differences for decades in his Love Lab. From extensive research, he has concluded that there are primary conflict styles that partners use with one another. Conflict styles are established by each individual's emotional development. As we just uncovered, we all learn from our families growing up how to deal with disagreements and the anger that accompanies them. Then based upon what we learn, we take those skills into our intimate relationships. Gottman has discovered that the couples who bring in similar conflict styles and conflict resolution skills have a more satisfying relationship than couples that come together with different conflict styles and resolution skills.

This seems obvious, yet problems with conflict often appear elusive to couples, similar styles or not. The spontaneous combustion that occurs when a couple fights can feel like a mysterious Bigfoot that comes out of the woods, wreaks havoc, and then retreats. Where did it come from, what is it, and when will we see it again? Partners are left confused and disoriented by the same person they proclaim to love and adore. But the truth is, how conflict plays out in a couple's relationship becomes quite predictable after the first year together. Gottman's research tells us that in a short period of time, couples find a stable pattern of negotiating conflict that will remain throughout their relationship.

Can You See Why Some Conflict Style Education Might Be Helpful?

It really is essential that you understand not only your preferred conflict style, but also your partner's conflict style. Greater insight on both of your parts can provide empathy for your similarities and differences during disagreements. This, in turn, can ease your conflicts simply because they become more intimately understood and no longer feel foreign and confusing like the mysterious Bigfoot. When we have insight into an experience, it offers us the opportunity to respond rather than react. So many couples exist in conflict hell because they spend their relationship reacting to their partner's conflict style during disagreements and trying to accommodate or resist it, rather than just accepting "This is how we do conflict together, so let's figure out how to do it well."

Moving forward, you will learn the different conflict styles typically at play in a couple's relationship. We will explore how the conflict styles can work together and how they can work against each other. And you will see how pursuing solutions regardless of personal style can be the ultimate path to conflict recovery.

Conflict Styles

Following are the five most commonly used conflict styles. Each style has a short description to help you understand what it may look like in action. The first three styles are referred to as "typical" because they are most often experienced in couple conflict interactions. The last two styles are referred to as "overreacting" as they are the result of an exaggerated emotional and physical experience. As you read the descriptions, the chances are high that you will identify with the style you are most prone to use and the style your partner uses. You may find that you use more than one style depending on the topic of conflict, or you may find that your conflict style is consistent no matter the content discussed. Furthermore, it may help you start to frame up the similarities and differences between you and your partner.

Typical Conflict Styles

The Discusser

When conflict arises, The Discusser likes to process thoughts and feelings through conversation. For this partner, solutions appear the more they are able to talk about what is going on. Furthermore, negative emotions start to evaporate as they are brought out into the open and dissected. When conflict is present, The Discusser is more than willing to say, "Can we talk?" or "Are you OK? Something seems off with us." This invitation is the start of emotional relief for The Discusser, who has a very hard time tolerating waiting for a resolution or avoiding the problem altogether. Not all Discussers are the same, however; some are very comfortable having emotional content drive the conversation, while others may prefer to package emotion in intellectual thoughts or a business mode of problem-solving. One similarity that all Discussers tend to share is the strong desire to pursue solutions and come to a resolution rather than allowing conflict to linger.

The Demander

In conflict, The Demander gets his or her thoughts and feelings out and doesn't mind a good fight. Emotions for this partner often feel like they are corked in a bottle of champagne. Once popped, the feelings spill over until they are all out in the open. This is a path to The Demander feeling relieved as processing emotions passionately is productive for them. The Demander wants to be heard. Demanders like their partner to meet them with a similar intensity of emotion as this equates to caring in their mind. Most of all, The Demander feels big and loves big, so when emotions enlarge, they typically feel validated and comfortable.

The Distancer

When engaging in conflict, The Distancer needs time to process what they think and feel before they can discuss things. Often more introspective or analytical, this partner cannot be pushed to process before they are ready. If asked to enter a conversation before they are prepared, they will retreat further like a turtle into a shell. Eventually, they may be willing to talk through differences but will do so with limited emotionality and, if met with a lot of poking and prodding, can slink back. Some Distancers may prefer to avoid conflicts altogether, allowing problems to resolve on their own, while others are more than willing to seek resolution but need time to think through things first. The Distancer likes to manage emotion in a quiet, controlled fashion and is rarely pushed to an emotional outburst.

Overreacting Conflict Styles

Humans are very predictable creatures when faced with fear. Pre-programmed to react in a self-preserving way, our operating system prompts us to flee, fight, or freeze when confronted with a threat. This, of course, is meant to happen in the presence of real, life-threatening danger. However, at times our wires get crossed, and we perceive imminent danger in non-life-threatening circumstances. A variety of names exist for what happens in the brain when this phenomenon occurs, including flooding, primitive brain reactivity, and amygdala highjack. They all refer to the same simple result: We overreact. We can experience an emotional overreaction through the blurring of thoughts, confusion, anxiety, or extreme anger, and we can overreact physically by running, shaking, crying, fighting, or shutting down while feeling our blood pressure rising. In this state, not only are we psychologically unable to process what is happening at the moment, but we are also physiologically unable to calm ourselves down. These are the two overreacting conflict styles:

The Disappearer

At the first sign of trouble, The Disappearer seeks to avoid all thoughts and feelings related to the conflict. If any tension is present, this partner is looking for the nearest door. That can be a real door: You may find him or her literally leaving the situation. Or it can be an emotional door where The Disappearer may escape, shutting down any possibility of conflict escalation. Disappearers cannot regulate the emotional and physical reactivity they experience when in conflict, and they find relief by withdrawing and leaving the situation behind. Over the years Disappearers have learned that it is safer to flee or freeze, allowing them to get away when things heat up.

The Destroyer

When overwhelmed with conflict, The Destroyer cannot tolerate the emotional and physical arousal of conflict and, in turn, lashes out in heightened anger. This behavior is in an attempt to both dump the emotional overload and shut down his or her partner so that the overwhelming reaction can go away. Often referred to as "seeing red," The Destroyer typically doesn't remember everything they said and did in this overreactive state. The Destroyer's struggle to regulate the mind and body results in a big fight, which from his or her perspective seems justified. From their partner's perspective, however, it appears destructive. The Destroyer believes that the only way out is to fight harder.

Both The Disappearer and The Destroyer are activated in conflict with a partner because his or her brain perceives greater danger than what is actually happening. We all may have this experience at times depending on the circumstances we are in with our partner. However, if a partner is consistently defaulting to The Disappearer or The Destroyer conflict style, it can indicate a deeper concern is driving him or her to this overwhelmed state. This could be because the experience is triggering a past traumatic memory or creating a sense of possible abandonment. It can also be the result of growing up in a chaotic family system that used abusive communication and forms of discipline. Typically, if a partner is overreacting this dramatically consistently, it isn't just because that's how he or she likes to manage conflict. Your relationship doesn't have to continue to suffer through these types of painful conflict interactions. This is a perfect reason to get some support from a couples therapist, which can be life changing for you, your partner, and the relationship.

Benefit of Similarity

After reviewing the different conflict styles, it may seem obvious that the process of conflict resolution is made much easier when couples approach it the same way. If you and your partner naturally tend to conflict with the same style, you may even feel like you don't have conflict in the relationship. You know you disagree at times, but the road to recovery is pretty smooth when you are moving at the same speed and in the same direction.

Where you lose benefits in similarity is when both of you consistently fall into overreacting conflict styles. If both of you are disappearing on each other, you will not reach a resolution, which offers critical recovery to a relationship. In similar fashion, if you are both destroying each other through conflict, it is only going to create bigger problems and hurts that will remain unresolved. Both of these styles wear down the relationship, similar or not.

Understanding Differences

Differences in conflict styles are usually at the root of the majority of a couple's discontent with their relationship. When couples talk about their relationship not working well, they often refer to having a "communication problem." Although communication skills such as listening and responding are critical to healthy relationships, most miscommunication occurs during negative experiences in the relationship or during conflict. Couples that approach conflict differently tend to feel misunderstood and unheard. This is often interpreted to mean that they lack communication skills. Yet when I have met many of these couples, I have observed that they communicate really well during regular, everyday interactions. What they don't do well with each other is fight and recover, not because they are missing good communication skills but because they approach managing anger and resolving conflict from an entirely different angle.

The Pursue/Distance Adaptation

Did you ever see a *Tom and Jerry* cartoon? *Tom and Jerry* is the Hanna-Barbera/MGM classic animated comedy of the cat-and-mouse game. Tom, the cat, spends episode after episode trying to catch Jerry, the crafty little mouse. Every time, it is the same story: Tom gets stirred up, Jerry escapes, and they spend the rest of the show irritating one another to no end. One of the primary outcomes of different conflict styles is the same irritating, never-ending feeling of the cat-and-mouse game. This game was originally defined by Virginia Satir, a pioneer in the field of relationship therapy, as the pursue/distance adaptation. Satir observed that when partners had different comfort levels with conflict engagement, they could not tolerate the same path to conflict resolution. So combining different conflict styles created an adaptive pattern of one partner pursuing resolution of their feelings, while the other partner created distance to prevent feeling overwhelmed. As one style moves closer, the other runs away. The chart below illustrates the pursue/distance adaptation that occurs when you mix the three typical conflict styles:

Style: The Demander Fighting with Style: The Discusser	• **The Demander** Pursues – "Where is your passion? Not everything is reasonable! Fight with me and I will know you really care." • **The Discusser** Distances – "This fighting is way too much for me. Can't we just be reasonable and talk about it?"
Style: The Discusser Fighting with Style: The Distance	• **The Discusser** Pursues – "I don't understand why you can't just talk about things with me? I feel so frustrated when you shut down." • **The Distancer** Distances – "Will you please give me some space to process things? Talking is just too much right now."
Style: The Demander Fighting with Style: The Distancer	• **The Demander** Pursues – "Why are you leaving me, don't you love me? Will you please just push back and show up!" • **The Distancer** Distances – "Go away and stop yelling at me. You make everything such a big deal and it is overwhelming."

(Please note that overreacting conflict styles can be substituted as *The Demander for The Destroyer* and *The Distancer for The Disappearer*, creating similar yet exaggerated reactions.)

As you can see, when couples have different conflict styles, it is common for them to end up chasing each other like Tom and Jerry in an attempt to find a resolution. This can naturally create increased frustration and emotional exhaustion. It can also reduce empathy for one another and allow partners to place further blame on each other. All of this added consternation happens just because couples have different ways of resolving conflict. To understand your relationship better, breakdown what you learned about conflict styles in your relationship with the following exercise:

{"Is This Normal?" Exercise}

CORE ELEMENT
Common Conflict Styles for
Committed Couples

My preferred conflict style is _____DYNHR_____.

My partner's preferred conflict style is _DISCuuu_.

Describe how your conflict styles work together. Are they similar or different?

DIF —> spon to DIIuis PRob AYHR could

Do you have *Tom and Jerry* moments in your conflicts? Explain what that looks like.

exon Vr cydn crys

What is one thing you can do differently in conflict now that you understand your style?

nothw.

What are the "chronic" conflict experiences (recurring arguments) in your relationship?

Spleen Mind

How do your conflict styles affect these disagreements?

Sens it

Learning to Fight Better

I get excited when couples come to see me and their primary concern is conflict. Why? Because conflict management is a learned skill. Most couples find relief in defining their conflict styles and understanding how they play out together in the relationship. After that, the next step is to learn how to fight better. Once this is accomplished, couple relationship satisfaction can increase substantially. Remaining happy together requires conflict resolution and, more importantly, conflict recovery. Finding our way back to each other and reconnecting after disagreements is critical for the couple relationship to survive and thrive. Therefore, pursuing solutions to conflict must transcend your style.

It is highly likely that you are going to continue to use your preferred conflict style, just as it is highly unlikely that you solve conflict in exactly the same way your partner prefers to. However, in adulthood, everything is open to positive change. The word *style* implies preference, not a fixed trait. So getting acquainted with your style, playing with it, and seeing how you can modify it is something you are capable of doing. The truth is, you will use your style differently when you are aware of what is going on between you and your partner.

This awareness can be referred to as the Matrix Effect. If you ever saw the *Matrix* movies, you may recall that Neo, the unsuspecting hero of the series, initially lived in the world unconscious of what was going on around him. He played along in the Matrix because he had no idea what he was reacting to or why. In a quintessential scene, Morpheus, one who had long understood the game, offered Neo a red pill or a blue pill. The blue pill would lull him back into the illusion of the Matrix, while the red pill was an opportunity to step into reality and lift the veil on what was really going on around him. Neo chose the red pill and stepped through the looking glass.

In choosing this paradigm shift, Neo began to see the Matrix for what it was, and the more he understood, the more he was able to control his destiny. That is what happens to couples when they become intimately aware of how they fight. A veil lifts. Their consciousness increases, and in turn, they are better able to control their experiences instead of unconsciously reacting or overreacting to each other. Together you can modify what you do in conflict and create different results. By choosing to work with your style and control the situation, you are invited to enter conflict at a new level, becoming a Humble Warrior in your relationship.

The Humble Warrior Explained

To be humble is to be low, putting others first. To be a warrior is to be assertive and persistent, to not give up. These two stances sit in juxtaposition to one another, yet they have been the key combination to any triumphant and sustainable revolution throughout history. Humble Warriors have stood out in history as strong yet gentle leaders who effectively created life-enhancing and sustainable change. Think of Gandhi or Martin Luther King Jr. These figures marked the world by confronting conflict with love and humility while also holding strong and not backing down. They were driven by their beliefs in an improved society—not just for themselves, but for everyone. When faced with massive differences, they declared there to be a better way where we all win. They embodied the definition of Humble Warrior.

In your world with your partner, you too can declare a better way and make a path for peace. Humility, assertiveness, and persistence are extremely valuable traits in our lives as well, particularly with those we love the most. If you want to create a revolution in your relationship, these are your critical partners. At this point you may be thinking, "That's all well and good, but I am no Gandhi or Martin Luther King Jr., and I have no idea how to be a Humble Warrior." Don't worry; we are going to walk through this one together. Let's take a look at some simple ways you can start to become a Humble Warrior in your relationship. Also, remember: We are not shooting for perfection. This is an invitation to step into health and happiness! Just give this a try. I think it will help.

Becoming a Humble Warrior

The late University of Southern California philosophy professor and theologian, Dallas Willard, PhD, offers a great definition of humility in his book *Hearing God*: "Refrain from *pretending* we are what we know we are not; *presuming* a favorable position for ourselves in any respect; [and] *pushing* or trying to override the will of others in our context." Not pretending, not presuming, and not pushing is an excellent framework for remodeling your thinking in conflict. Regardless of your conflict styles, you can choose to pursue solutions in the following way:

Stop Pretending That . . .

- *Your way is the only or best way.* If you are in a relationship with another person, there are always going to be two ways to do something. In actuality, there are more than two, but the point is that there is more than just *your* way. Don't get stuck on yourself.

- *You are right and the other person is wrong.* This is a very black-and-white way of seeing the world and your partner. Consider this: In a relationship with another person who loves you, is there ever any value in making him or her wrong? In doing so, you shut down the person they are and shut off your ability to learn.

- *You are blameless.* Blame is a dangerous way to approach your partner. I have never met a person who, when blamed for something, responded positively or cooperatively. Would you?

- *Your style is the best way to process conflict.* If you have read this chapter, you know this isn't true. This is a very egotistical stance and doesn't allow for empathy to exist.

Stop Presuming That . . .

- *You have all the information.* You may know all there is to know about a situation, but what if you don't? Just maybe there is more information that could be critical to the issue at hand and change your whole view on things. Shutting yourself off to curiosity can hurt you.

- *You need or want different outcomes.* If you enter a conflict with this belief, it will keep you from the creative problem-solving process that can eventually lead to a win-win.

- *You know how this conflict ends.* Over time, it can be easy to slip into the assumption that all fights go the same way. When you enter a conflict from this position, chances are very high that you will get what you are asking for rather than shifting your behavior to create a new outcome.

Stop Pushing For . . .

- *Your partner to make the first move.* Life is short; why be passive, especially in the relationship that matters the most? It is a loving act to pursue peace.

- *Your partner to change.* Keep in mind, if you think it is so easy for someone else to change to please you, then it should be equally as easy for you to change to please him or her.

- *Your partner to understand you.* Sometimes to be understood, you need to understand. Step into your partner's shoes, and see if you can identify with what blocks his or her understanding. Can you help your partner understand rather than demanding to be understood?

The final key to not pretending, presuming, and pushing is found in understanding where your real power lies in a relationship. The opposite of being humble is being egotistical or having an inflated sense of self. It is this ego state that is at work in all of the Drama patterns. The ego likes to overcome others because this act affirms that it is better than others. This is an illusion of power that pumps up self-importance while diminishing everyone else.

True power exists in understanding yourself and your strengths and weaknesses enough to set yourself aside for the greater good. In this real state of humility, there is such confidence in who you are that you never need to prove it to anyone, much less the one you have given full, intimate access to. From this position, you are free to be wrong, offer apologies, say that another is right, ask for forgiveness, and let go—the ultimate form of freedom.

The Humble Warrior Challenge

Try walking this humble path in your conflicts. Pick a chronic or recurring conflict in your relationship, and answer the questions on the Humble Warrior Approach that follow. *Be honest* with yourself. So often, we are frustrated with a problem that we haven't put any real solutions to yet. We want things to change but really aren't ready to make any changes. There is a big gap between wanting and doing. Sometimes we are so frustrated with our partner that we put our heels in the ground and decide we aren't going to move anywhere until the other person moves. This is a guaranteed way to stay miserable. Happiness is a choice, and if you're not pursuing it (which is your right), it's on you. Think about how you can pursue happiness without waiting for your partner. We all like to be surprised and delighted in our relationships. Implementing solutions without being asked is a way to let your partner know that you are paying attention and are willing to show up for the relationship.

Don't give up! If you make changes in how you approach conflict and it doesn't work, try again. Engage your partner, and let him or her know how you are attempting to change. Let your partner know that you aren't perfect and you aren't going to stop trying to figure things out. This is how you allow the warrior to rise up and stay in the battle.

The Humble Warrior Approach to Conflict

Answer the following questions *honestly*. When you are done, your path to action will be clear. Then, take what you have learned and discuss it with your partner. If the conversation escalates, take a break, cool down, read this chapter one more time, and try again.

1. What is an outstanding conflict in your relationship that needs attention?

2. How long has this conflict been around? Is it chronic or reoccurring in your relationship?

3. Is this conflict about a fundamental difference in values that will not change but needs to move toward acceptance?

4. Stepping into your partner's shoes, what solutions does your partner believe would address the situation or make things better?

5. What are *two or more* solutions you know might make a difference, but you haven't tried to date?

6. Now, honestly, why haven't you tried any of the potential solutions in answers 4 and 5? You have solutions to your problems. What are the obstacles keeping you from these solutions?

7. How are you pretending, presuming, and/or pushing in this conflict, preventing progress from happening, or maintaining the obstacles to solutions? (Look back at the definitions if you need to.)

Pretending:

Presuming:

Pushing:

8. How do your conflict styles contribute to not pursuing solutions? How can you approach this conflict differently with your conflict styles in mind?

9. Knowing all of this information, can you show up as a Humble Warrior in your relationship? What steps are you going to take to change the situation today?

(Dr. Pete Pearson and Dr. Ellyn Bader at The Couples Institute in California inspired the above questionnaire. They are rock star couples therapists with a genuine passion for their work. If you are in their area, I highly suggest their clinics or events.)

5

Lesson from Viktor

Congratulations—you have finished the Core Elements and are ready to start in on the Mind Benders and Muscle Builders! The following information will be really helpful to know before you start practicing the Mind Bender and Muscle Builder exercises. Earlier in chapter 1, I introduced you to the cognitive-behavioral concept, which explains how what you believe about your life drives what you think, what you think about your life drives how you feel, and ultimately what you feel about your life creates your reactions, in turn affecting your experiences. Here is a simple example: If you believe your life is great, you think good things about your life, generating happy feelings and positive experiences. However, if you believe your life is awful, you think bad things about your life, producing unhappy feelings and negative experiences.

One of the most substantial writings on this concept can be found in Viktor Frankl's classic book, *Man's Search for Meaning*. Frankl was a Jewish German psychiatrist, neurologist, and professor who endured the savage genocide during World War II, losing those he loved and spending years in concentration camps. Remarkably, he survived and lived to write about the amazing capacity of the human mind to overcome the greatest of evil. His understanding is best expressed in his writing when he says, "Everything can be taken from a man but one thing: the last of the human freedoms—to choose one's attitude in any given set of circumstances, to choose one's own way." The power we hold to self-regulate our inner world and, in turn, communicate our experiences to the outside world is not only in our control, but also is our true freedom. What is really outstanding is our innate ability to adjust our experiences by learning how to shift our beliefs, work with our thoughts, manage our emotions, and effectively change our communication.

Although there are physical and mental illnesses that can inhibit modifying our thoughts and moods, for the majority of people, increasing this skill is possible in every moment of every day. What it requires is time, attention, and discipline—just like getting physically fit or establishing financial stability.

Two Scales: Inside and Outside

Surprisingly, learning how to have a better relationship doesn't start with understanding each other. It starts with understanding yourself, specifically, how well you manage and communicate your own thoughts and emotions. To do that, it can be really beneficial to complete a personal assessment of where you land on The Inside Scale and The Outside Scale. The Inside Scale assesses your ability to understand and manage your own emotional experiences: what is going on inside your head and heart. This can also be referred to as self-regulation. The Outside Scale assesses your ability to communicate your emotional experiences in a clear and concise way: how well you are able to take what is going on inside your head and heart and communicate it to your partner. This can also be referred to as self-disclosure. When working in a relationship with another person, your ability to process and control your own emotions and then, in turn, articulate them in a way someone else can process and understand is the key to healthy and productive communication. Never is this type of communication more necessary than when in an intimate relationship with another person.

Let's take a look at the two scales, and you can assess for yourself where you land. Most of us are pretty well aware of our strength and growth areas. However, if you are unsure, getting some feedback from your partner or a friend who knows you well can be helpful. Read through the examples below, and then mark on the scale where you think your skill level is *most* of the time. If there is a specific topic, concern, or event that takes you to a different area on the scale, make a note of that also.

The Inside Scale
How Well Can I Self-Regulate My Emotional Experiences?

(Read through the descriptions below, and mark where you think you land on this scale.)

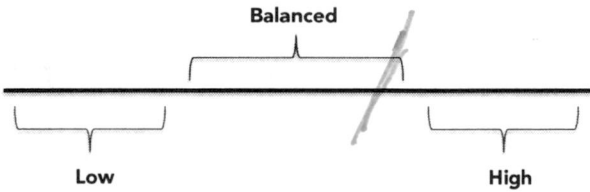

Low self-regulation. Low self-regulation means that you are unconscious of or struggle to understand your emotional reactions. Emotions feel like they come out of nowhere and are the result of external sources: other people "make" you feel a certain way, or circumstances cause your emotions to occur. You do not control your emotional experiences, and you often blame your reactions and behavior on how you feel. Emotions happen to you, and you cannot manage where they come from or their outcome. Do emotions pop out of nowhere for you? Do you attribute the origins of your feelings to others or the world around you? *Mark low on the scale.*

Balanced self-regulation. Balanced self-regulation exists when you have a firm understanding of your emotional experiences and can manage them well. You are aware that emotions reside inside of you and are connected to what you believe about the world. When emotions arise, you meet them confidently and can process where they originated from and what they mean to you and to your experiences. Also you can delineate the contributing experiences, relationships, and environmental factors that trigger your beliefs and instigate your emotional reactions. Do you find that you can identify how you feel, understand where it is coming from for you, and then process it accordingly? *Mark balanced on the scale.*

High self-regulation. High self-regulation occurs when you overanalyze your thoughts and emotions. You have moved beyond understanding and are internalizing your thoughts and emotions in a way that causes you to be paralyzed or shut down. You second-guess your reactions, feel overly responsible for every emotion you have, and/or may be highly sensitive to emotional experiences. As a result, you may minimize or exaggerate your feelings internally, becoming trapped trying to make sense of them before you look to any relational or external impacts that contribute to your personal experience. Do you get stuck with your emotions in a paralysis of analysis? *Mark high on the scale.*

As you read through the range of The Inside Scale, can you identify your place on the continuum? This is meant to be a generalized assessment of how you typically manage your emotional experiences. As you thought through this evaluation, did you land somewhere in between these reactions, depending on the emotions you are experiencing? Do you find that certain events or circumstances move you to different places on the scale? Once you understand where you land, you can start to work with your "inside" experience differently. If you fall consistently on either end of the scale, you may find it negatively affects the quality of your relationship and can serve as an indication that you need to work on bringing your self-regulation to a more balanced state. Only you can do this for yourself; your partner cannot balance your emotions for you. They may help you co-regulate by processing your thoughts and feelings with you, but it is ultimately up to you to manage your inner world.

The Outside Scale
How Well Do I Self-Disclose My Emotional Experiences?

(Once again, read through the descriptions below, and mark where you think you land on this scale.)

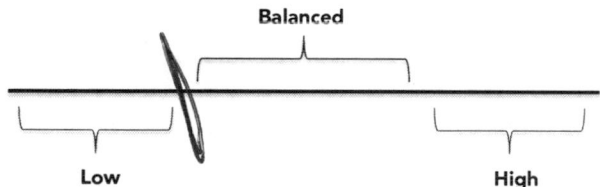

Low self-disclosure. Low self-disclosure occurs when you are too cautious with your communication, afraid that anything you say will be misinterpreted or misunderstood. Possibly, you cannot find the right words to express your emotional experience and, as a result, get tongue-tied and say nothing. You may also find yourself practicing what to say over and over again in your mind but then unable to tell your partner out loud. Or, you may lack the desire to communicate, preferring to keep to yourself primarily. Do you get stuck in your head and find the words hard to come by or the message too difficult to get across? *Mark low on the scale.*

Balanced self-disclosure. Balanced self-disclosure means you have carefully thought through your emotional experience and are able to identify what is necessary and valuable to communicate and what is not. You may even desire to say something impulsive, but you hold back because you know it will not benefit or move the conversation forward in a positive direction. Also, you may not want to say anything and just hope your partner can figure it out, but you know you are responsible for sharing what you think and feel; no one is capable of reading your mind. Do you find you tend to think through your inside experience and attempt to share in a way that benefits your relationship? *Mark balanced on the scale.*

High self-disclosure. High self-disclosure exists when it is tough for you to control your communication, especially during emotional experiences. When you feel, you automatically express without even considering the impact your communication will have on others. You have a very hard time managing the impulse to say whatever is on your mind. Often this creates more problems in relationships, and you may find yourself regretting what you said after the fact. Do you typically just say whatever is on your mind without thinking ahead? *Mark high on the scale.*

After reviewing the different positions on The Outside Scale, do you have an idea of where you would line up? Again, this is meant to be a simple way to identify what your typical experience is and how you might benefit from improvement. Are certain issues or topics harder to disclose or contain than others in your relationship? Identifying these specific areas can be really helpful moving forward. It might be that you are communicating to your partner what is going on inside of you really well, with the exception of a tender or aggravating topic. These would be areas you could address. Again, operating the majority of the time at either end of this scale is going to cause problems in your relationship. You will want to work on bringing yourself to a more balanced place to increase relationship satisfaction.

A Greater Goal

The simple statement "Know thyself" is a widely known ancient Greek aphorism often attributed to Socrates. Centuries later, the words continue to hold singular relevance for humanity. Getting a grasp of how you process and communicate your emotional experiences is an invitation to "know thyself." This pursuit alone can significantly improve your relationship. Self-regulation and self-disclosure are both "know thyself" muscles that will be strengthened throughout the rest of this book. You can learn how to regulate your emotions in a moderate and balanced way by working with your thoughts, feelings, and beliefs. You can become a good emotional communicator by practicing assertiveness, shared meanings, and active listening skills. Your relationship only gets better as you work these muscles. Everyone can benefit from this work in life. The following Mind Benders and Muscle Builders are going to take you through a variety of exercises that work on the inside and the outside experiences in your individual life and in your relationship together. Each one will offer an opportunity for you to increase your skills and abilities while providing a way to practice with your partner by following this formula:

INSIGHT + ACTION + PRACTICE = POSITIVE CHANGE

Then look out, because by the time you and your partner are done, your relationship will experience a revolution!

MIND BENDERS
Be the Change in Your Relationship

Mind Benders are exercises that challenge you as an individual to be the change you wish to see in the relationship. You don't have the power to change your partner, but you do have the power to change yourself. The more you are able to work within yourself to understand and manage your thoughts and feelings, the better your relationship will be. When both you and your partner work on these skills, the progress can be remarkable!

INSIGHT + ACTION + PRACTICE = POSTIVE CHANGE

6

Stopping the Train

Insight

Did you know that thoughts move through our brain like trains on a track? Really, it's true! All of our processing moves through the mind like little trains running efficiently down the tracks controlling how we think, feel, behave, and interact. Each of our trains of thought has its own unique track as the brain works to control between fifty and seventy thousand connections daily. Your brain is one busy place. Every connecting thought makes an impact on our functioning, but you need to know that the thoughts we have most frequently build the most-used tracks. Current neuroscience helps us understand this phenomenon by explaining that our most frequent or habitual thoughts become "grooved" into our brains, meaning they are more embedded in our brain than our less-frequent thoughts. These embedded grooves become the train tracks that our thoughts can get stuck on day in and day out.

Research also confirms that human beings can control what trains of thought become grooved by changing frequent unwanted thoughts with new, more desirable ways of thinking. This is because the brain is like a muscle and, like all other muscles in the body, can be manipulated to operate in ways we prefer it to. For example, if you want big biceps, you would lift weights focusing on your upper arm muscles. Over time, with this focused workout, your biceps would change and grow. Our brains are similar; if you want to adjust your thinking, you need to work out your thoughts to build new "grooves" or train tracks in your brain. This concept is explained well by Dr. Daniel Amen, a psychiatrist, brain health enthusiast, and author of *Change Your Brain, Change Your Life*, who has produced incredible research and education on the brain. Dr. Amen proposes that you can not only change your thoughts, but you can also change the actual physical structure of your brain through a brain workout. He says that mastering a brain workout creates positive results that can be very satisfying not just for you personally, but also for your couple relationship. Let's take a look at why this may be the case.

When we decide there is a problem in our relationship or a problem with our partner, it can be hard not to make that the focus of our attention. Often we can go on and on in our minds thinking about all of the reasons things are bad and why we are the victim of our partner's ridiculous behavior. This frequent use of negative thoughts builds train tracks that become easier and easier to access as we think negatively about our partner. Before we know it, our train of thought is moving quickly and frequently to a place where we can't stand our relationship, and we feel awful. Neuroscience research confirms this experience too. Dr. Rick Hanson, author of *Buddha's Brain: The Practical Neuroscience of Happiness, Love, and Wisdom*, says that our brains are Velcro for negative experiences and Teflon for positive experiences. The brain is sticky with the negative thoughts and stores them as future reminders of what we should avoid. This means that if you don't intentionally manage your thinking when you are feeling negative about your partner, your brain will eventually be full of "grooved" tracks, moving along more of the negative experiences in your relationship instead of the positive. Once you get to this place, couples research tells us that relationships overcome by negative feelings struggle to stay satisfying and threaten a couple's longevity together. This would indicate that working with negative feelings and thoughts right away, rather than letting them accumulate, is not only a good brain workout, but is also essential if we want to remain happily together. The catch is that you are the only one who can switch your train of thought. Your partner cannot do this for you.

Action

If you want to turn your negative thinking around, you need to become a train stopper. When you hear your thoughts starting to chug to Negativeville about your partner, tell yourself, "*Stop!*" Think of a big, flashing red light and a clanging bell of warning. It's time to stop the train, pull the switch, and put your thoughts on a new track. The only way to do this is by engaging in a brain workout. Here's how you do that.

Shifting your train of negative thought starts by getting to the bottom of what you believe about any negative circumstance in your relationship. Once you can identify what you believe, you have the amazing power to change your experiences. So often our beliefs contain misinformation, assumptions, unclear thinking, and mistruths. We must question our beliefs to adjust how we feel. Here is an example to illustrate how: Let's say you find yourself feeling upset with your partner because they forgot to take out the trash. You start thinking to yourself, "Man, my partner is forgetful; they can't follow through with anything! As a matter of fact, they are selfish. And, you know what, if they really cared about me, they would have remembered. This is just *another* example of how they don't care." Each of these thoughts is building grooves in your brain and contains negative beliefs about your partner. It is important to know that your beliefs will remain valid and in place until you address them. They will not change unless you work them out. So what can you do to change your thinking and shift your beliefs so that by the time your partner gets home you don't lay into him or her and ruin your evening together? The best way to do this workout is by breaking down each thought and then restating it with either *clarity* or an *action step*. Notice how helpful it is to look at each negative train of thought individually and work it out to create a new train track.

Negative Train of Thought: My Partner Is Forgetful

Stop! Now break it down to change tracks:

- *Clarity option.* My partner is forgetful sometimes; this is a part of who they are, and I can live with it.

- *Action option.* I wonder if my partner had a lot on his/her mind this morning; it is not like him/her to forget. Maybe I should check in and find out what's going on.

Negative Train of Thought: My Partner Can't Follow through with Anything

Stop! Now break it down to change tracks:

- *Clarity option.* My partner struggles to follow through with tasks, but sometimes I do too. I guess we are not perfect.

- *Action option.* Maybe I need to stop expecting my partner to do something he/she will never do. We need to make a different plan for taking out the trash if it bothers me this much.

Negative Train of Thought: My Partner Is Selfish

Stop! Now break it down to change tracks:

- *Clarity option.* I know my partner isn't selfish; I think I am embellishing a bit because I am irritated.

- *Action option.* If I really feel like my partner is selfish, I better talk to him/her about that because I don't want to keep feeling this bad.

Negative Train of Thought: My Partner Doesn't Care about Me

Stop! Now break it down to change tracks:

- *Clarity option.* I know my partner cares about me. This thought is really dramatic and unnecessary.

- *Action option.* I guess I need to remind my partner that I feel cared for and loved when he/she remembers to do things around the house.

This brain workout is fairly simple to do, and, like any good physical conditioning, it requires you to take dedicated time and focus. After you have created your new tracks, be sure to keep your train of thought on them, and don't switch back to the original negative thinking tracks. By maintaining your new thinking, you will shift your beliefs, change how you feel, and create new, positive grooves that you can access in the future. A helpful hint to consider is the more you pay attention to what you are telling yourself and practice shifting your thinking, the easier it gets. When you take immediate action to shift your negative thoughts, you will proactively reset beliefs that could undermine your relationship and, in turn, build positive thoughts to encourage and support your relationship. Want to get really good at stopping your negative trains of thought and building new tracks? Use the Train-Stopping Brain Workout provided below.

{Reset Your Negative Train of Thought Exercise}

MIND BENDER
Train-Stopping Brain Workout

1. What are the negative feelings I have about my partner or relationship?

2. Name your emotions. What happened to trigger these feelings about my partner or relationship?

   Describe the circumstance.

Now complete the next two steps to break down and adjust your thinking. (Use the "My partner forgot to take out the trash" example if it helps you.)

1. What am I telling myself about what happened? What do I believe about my partner or relationship in my negative circumstance? Write down your negative trains of thought:

2. How clear is my thinking? What thoughts need clarity, or what actions do I need to take to help stop the train and build new tracks? Break down your negative trains of thought, and create options for your new tracks. The following is to help you get started:

My Negative Train of Thought:

Stop! Now break it down to change tracks:

Clarity option. *[handwritten]*

Action option. *[handwritten]*

Once you have a breakdown list, determine what you need to do. This could include changing a long-held negative belief about your partner, shifting your expectations, talking through the issue with your partner in a non-blaming way, or anything else that helps you build a new positive train track for your thoughts.

How Will Train-Stopping Revolutionize Your Relationship?

Imagine a relationship that isn't carrying the extra weight of negativity. Instead of letting negative thinking take control of your relationship, you will take over your own mind. By doing so, you will save yourself from many unnecessary train rides! You will breathe new life into your relationship when you stop the negative train-of-thought accumulation, creating more time to focus on what really matters and fostering positive feelings in the relationship. This is good preventive medicine for you and your relationship long term.

7

A Loving Observer

Insight

When we are all worked up in our relationship, it is typically a result of using judgments or forming authoritative opinions that are conclusive and don't allow room for negotiation. Sometimes these judgments are based on fact; however, more often they are determined by our feelings. You may feel disregarded, disrespected, or unloved by your partner and come to firm conclusions about him or her and, in turn, your relationship. It is like you put on a black robe, sit on a big bench, and hit the gavel, making a resolute decision about how your relationship will be from here on out. When you approach your relationship from the seat of judgment, interactions and conversations become rigid and controlling. This causes negative feelings to elevate and can leave you standing in the middle of an emotional tornado. From this perspective, everything swirls around you, creating confusion and requiring quick reactions rather than reasoned responses. Thoughts like "This isn't the way things work" or "You can't do or say that" may surface as the Judge in you attempts to bring the chaos to order. Well, news flash—no one likes the feeling of being judged.

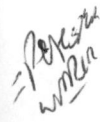

The alternative to using the role of Judge is to become a Loving Observer. Rather than creating a firm, conclusive opinion, a Loving Observer approaches from a position of curiosity. The primary goal of the Loving Observer is to explore and understand as an act of love toward your partner. The Loving Observer position helps you to be curious about your partner's thoughts and actions, where he or she is coming from, where he or she is headed, and how you might avoid future troubles. Looking at your relationship from this distance and with love can create some compassion for what is going on for you and your partner. This is a really helpful way to step out of judgment. When you feel the swirl of emotions trying to draw you in, get curious and decide to become a Loving Observer.

Action

Judgment is an easy position to put ourselves in, because it holds great power and protects our fears. If I am right, then even if you hurt me, I still win. This is a position of the Ego, self-preserving and demanding. This exercise isn't going tell you to stop judging; it is going to ask you to exchange judgment for curiosity, much the same way you might offer a child an apple instead of a candy bar. The candy bar may taste superb, but, in the long run, the apple is a better choice. In this case, wherever you are holding judgments about your partner or relationship, you are going to exchange them for curiosity. Here is an example for you:

The Sponge Story

I met Sam and Tammie five months before their wedding. They were a very sincere, friendly couple, and I knew early on that they seemed to be a good match for one another. We spent our time together discussing everything pertinent for a couple to cover before making a lifelong commitment. In our conversation, they both communicated well and shared keen insights on the relationship, their viewpoints, and most importantly, each other. At this point, they had been living together for about nine months, which means they had plenty of time to transition through the positives and negatives of becoming a "We" couple. This had been an especially challenging time for them initially as they both were in their midthirties and had spent a number of years living on their own. One day we began talking about how they managed household tasks, and Sam said to Tammie, "Should we tell her about the sponge?" I, of course, said, "Yes—please tell me about the sponge." This is the story that ensued.

There was a sponge on the kitchen sink. It was very important to Sam that the sponge was wrung dry in the morning before they left for work so that it wouldn't smell at the end of the day. Tammie often didn't wring out the sponge when she was the last person to leave, and this was very frustrating to Sam. As you can imagine, there was more than one fight about the smelly sponge at the end of the day, and Sam couldn't understand why Tammie wouldn't just wring out the stupid thing. Tammie didn't understand why in the world this was such a big deal to Sam. Both Sam and Tammie were firmly committed to judging the other. Sam judged there was a "right" way to handle a sponge. Tammie judged his reaction as ridiculous. At this point, I had Sam and Tammie take off their black robes and put on their lab coats.

> "Let's get curious and take a look at what is really going on here," I said. I asked Sam how he felt when he came home to a smelly sponge.
>
> "Mad," he responded.
>
> "OK," I said, "and what else?"
>
> "Well, hurt," he replied. Just then, Tammie took notice,

and I saw her expression shift from irritated to inquisitive.

"Why hurt, Sam?" I asked.

"Because I have asked her so many times, and I feel like she is doing this on purpose just to prove a point or something. Doesn't she care about me?" he asked. Tammie started getting tears in her eyes.

"What's going on for you, Tammie?" I asked.

"Well, I feel so bad because I do care, Sam. But you know how I grew up. My mom is so perfectionistic; there was always a right way to do everything. I am so afraid of living my life that way that sometimes I just leave the sponge in the morning to prove to myself that I am not like her. It is never meant to hurt you," she said.

At this point, Sam was looking right at her, his eyes welling up, and I may as well have left the room.

Both Sam and Tammie, by becoming curious, learned incredibly important facts about a common, everyday occurrence that was annoying their relationship. If this hadn't been uncovered, they would have continued to hold the incident against each other, building resentment through the years. Instead, through the power of shifting from Judge to Loving Observer, this couple connected on a level that radically changed their experience together permanently while also using a skill that will come in handy over and over again. And to think: all of this growth occurred because of a sponge.

A Loving Observer reserves judgment to be open to all the possibilities that are yet unknown. It is your turn to try this in your relationship. Visualize a big brown paper bag. Now, in your mind, collect all of the judgments you have about your partner. Think about the labels you put on them, such as too neat, sloppy, forgetful, anal, obsessive, silly, unresponsive, etc. Now, I want you to take your pile of judgments, big or small, and place them in the big brown paper bag. You don't need them right now. Next, answer the following questions. Then sit down with your partner and do some research. See if you can understand your partner better in an open, Loving Observer way.

{Reset Your Judgements}

MIND BENDER
Become a Loving Observer

1. What is a "sponge" issue or frustrating circumstance in your relationship?

2. Where are you being a Judge in this circumstance? What are you so sure you are right about?

3. How can you become a Loving Observer in this circumstance? What do you need to become more curious about?

4. Here are three types of questions a Loving Observer asks. Use these prompts with your "sponge" issue:

What don't I know about this circumstance?

What might be motivating this circumstance?

Knowing what I now know, how can I approach this circumstance differently than I have before?

How Will Being a Loving Observer Revolutionize Your Relationship?

When you let go of judgment, you free yourself up to understand your partner in a brand-new way. Curiosity is the lifeline to being vitally engrossed in the world and in your relationship. Relationships can change radically over the simplest of issues if we are willing to drop the Judge and become a Loving Observer.

8

The Small Big Things

Insight

It is amazing how often we leave the person we claim to care the most about out in the cold emotionally. There are multiple opportunities throughout the day for us to turn our attention to our partner and offer a loving touch, a word of encouragement, or even a friendly smile. But when relationships get worn out or life gets busy, often these moments are some of the first to go. Being selfless in a relationship is hard work. Learning how to balance sharing yourself and taking care of yourself is a constant task. However, maintaining a loving, connected relationship requires partners to choose each other, intentionally.

According to research, Relationship Self-Regulation, meaning how much couples pay attention to and work on their relationship, is directly correlated with long-term satisfaction. Just like your individual ability to self-regulate by managing your inner emotional experience effectively enhances your relationship, so does your ability to maintain your focus on the relationship and take action toward making it better. I know, this doesn't really seem like rocket science, but think of it this way: You probably also know that eating a balanced diet high in veggies and low in sugar can increase your health and decrease your weight. This is also proven through research. But do you do it consistently, on a daily basis?

Often we *know* what makes things better. It is moving the knowing into consistent action where we falter. There are typically two parts in us: One part is telling us what we "should do," trying to protect us from our fears, and the other part is justifying why we don't have to, in an attempt to comfort us. Actually, neither part is working in our relationship's best interest. What you need to access is your higher self in the relationship—the part that understands the bigger picture and realizes that the good feelings of connection, kindness, and compassion come when you attend to your partner and the relationship.

Studies on Relationship Self-Regulation confirm that a partner's satisfaction greatly increases when he or she feels their significant other's effort toward the relationship. Just knowing that the other person is working for the greater good makes the other partner want to engage also. That is a little like saying, "It's the thought that counts." Basically, if your partner can see your intentions are for him or her, the actual actions are just icing on the cake.

Action

Focusing your attention on your partner can be very simple. As a matter of fact, it is often the easy, daily, thoughtful acts that make the biggest impact. So, if you want to reengage your partner, do it in little ways: pour him or her a cup of coffee when you're filling your own; offer a gentle touch on the back or a kiss on the cheek when you walk by them; look at your partner, and tell them that they are hot or beautiful; send them a text to let them know you are thinking of them, wish them luck in a big meeting, or hope that they make it through a stressful day; or do one of the simplest actions these days:

when you are talking to each other or crawling into bed, put your phone away and give them 100 percent of you.

It is easy to pass these moments by, especially when we are busy in life or feeling discouraged in our relationship. But little moments really matter. These are the small big things that add up over time. After months and years of not offering intentional attention, we can create chasms of distance that are difficult to bridge. Build a "Small Big Things" list for your partner; what can you start doing today that will make a difference? Now, just do it.

{Reset Your Attention}

MIND BENDER

The Small Big Things List

Brainstorm here: What are some little ways you can turn your attention toward your partner? What would your partner appreciate? *— Love things*
— Texting things prep.
Write down two things you are going to start doing immediately: *Come things or te m*

Was it hard to make this list? (circle below)

> YES—You need to talk to your partner about what he or she likes and how he or she feels loved.
>
> NO—What keeps you from acting on this list?
>
> Identify your obstacles, and move them.

Remember—your partner can be a great resource. Ask them what you can do that helps them feel important and cared for.

How Will the Small Big Things Revolutionize Your Relationship?

Shifting your attention and taking small, deliberate actions toward your partner will increase your interest in the relationship. When couples start paying attention to each other, the natural by-product is a stronger connection that feels great. Remaining attentive to each other is like putting gas in the relationship tank: Keep it full, and you won't find your relationship stranded on the side of the road.

9

Releasing Expectations

Insight

Most of life's disappointments are directly connected to unmet expectations, especially in our closest relationships. The trouble with expectations is that they seem to be permanent residents in our mind when, in actuality, we create them. Dr. Albert Ellis was one of the funniest and most brilliant psychologists I have ever heard speak. His theory of rational emotive behavior therapy explains that we all have built expectations in our minds of how others "should be" or how things "must" happen in our relationships. Some of these expectations serve us well because they define healthy signs of respect and love, while other expectations are causing persistent conflict in our relationships because they are desires, not requirements. Dr. Ellis would often say, "Stop shoulding on things," or "Stop musterbating." He had a frank and amusing way of telling people to stop the very behaviors that were causing them so much grief.

Couples in long-term, satisfying relationships seem to have figured this out. One thing they all have in common is that they understand that their partner has limits to who they are, who they may become, and what they are capable of. This is not denying potential but rather accepting reality. The longer you "expect" your partner to be different than who he or she is, the more drawn-out your inner and external conflict will be. Resisting the reality of who your partner is entrenches your expectations and leads to constant disappointment. Expectations create resistance, and resistance rarely serves us well. When we are pushing against our partner, wanting him or her to change, it takes a lot of negative energy. You end up putting up walls that build distance between you.

Action

Right now, at this moment, you can let go of an expectation you have been holding onto that is keeping you captive. After all, you made it up in your mind. What is a limit that your partner has that continually brings you disappointment? Are they late a lot, forgetful, anxious, need consistency, like too much variety? Try accepting one of your partner's limits, and release your expectation that they will change.

Often it is helpful to delineate between Deal Breakers, Annoying Behaviors, and Personal Limits. Deal Breakers are behaviors that need to change because they are destroying the relationship. These things are not limits you would accept. Annoying Behaviors are actions your partner takes that really bother you, and it is important that you are talking about it if you haven't before. It may be something they would consider changing if they understood the problems it caused, but it also may be a limit you are unaware of. Personal Limits are parts of your partner's personality or way of living in the world that may be difficult for you to work with at times. However, these are the very behaviors that you need to consider accepting as a part of the whole package your partner brings.

Using a position of Loving Observer can be really helpful when accepting your partner's limits. Adopting a position of curiosity about your expectations and observing your partner's motivations and actions in love will allow you to step away from overpersonalizing. When you overpersonalize, you believe it is all about you and that your partner is out to get you with their behavior. Nine times out of ten it isn't about you at all; it is really about what is going on with your partner and how he or she is trying to manage his or her experience in the world. When we are able to look through the lens of a Loving Observer, we are able to see the difference, release our expectations, and accept our partners for who they are and not who we think they should be.

Oh, and guess what: You also have limits that are difficult for your partner to live with. Do you know what they are? There is always a quid pro quo in a long-term relationship, meaning a give-and-take or "You scratch my back, I'll scratch yours." Share your limits with each other, and have a sense of humor about it. After all, being human is quite comical. Then together decide to release expectations and increase acceptance of each other's faults and flaws.

{Reset Your Expectations}

MIND BENDER
Accepting Limits

Deal Breakers: (These behaviors are hurtful to the relationship and need to be addressed immediately.)

Annoying Behaviors: (These behaviors will cause problems if left unattended over time.)

Personal Limits: (These behaviors are a part of who your partner is and will not change, even if you keep trying.)

How can you reframe your partner's limits so you can accept "what is" rather than resisting who he or she is?

What do you think your limits are that are difficult for your partner to live with?

How Will Releasing Expectations Revolutionize Your Relationship?

Relationships are easier to be a part of when you aren't spending so much energy on resisting your partner. You and your partner will have more fun with each other when you can accept one another more freely. Having a sense of humor about your own foibles rather than being defensive really helps! When you stop resisting what is and accept the reality of your partner as he or she is, you will experience your relationship in a brand-new way.

10

Becoming More Critical

Insight

Do you know what most people are looking for when they come to see a couples therapist? Nope, not solutions to their problems. And no, not even better communication. Believe it or not, most people are looking for the therapist to collude with them and confirm that their criticism of their partner is accurate. This is really similar to when siblings fight and then go to a parent and say, "But guess what she did . . ." while waiting for the parent to say, "You did *what*? How could you do that?" We all have criticisms of our partners that would flourish with the affirmation from an authoritative third party. It's just that typically it doesn't make anything better. On the contrary, it tends to make things worse.

However, there is a type of criticism that really does help couples out. This is called Pre-Talk Thought. Pre-Talk Thought occurs when each partner does a *critical examination* of their own thoughts and feelings in preparation for a dialogue with their partner. Many difficulties in couple relationships originate from lack of critical thought before a conversation, particularly emotionally sensitive ones. And there is a perfectly common reason for this.

First, I want you to know that one of the greatest gifts you can give your partner is empathy. Empathy is the softening skill that combines compassion with understanding. We tend to be really good at this at the beginning of the relationship as we are wooing the other person to love and trust us. However, as time goes on, we often become more concerned about being understood. We lose the intense interest in getting underneath how our partner ticks, and instead we look for clues that they understand where we are coming from. It is really important that you see the essential role empathy plays. Without empathy, we become quite selfish, and this next action requires very vulnerable, unselfish choices.

So, let's get back to the perfectly common reason that most difficulties between couples occur when we are not thinking critically. Our brain typically works this way: We have a top thought and a base thought. The top thought is our reaction (what we feel safe saying or what we think will accomplish our goal and get us what we want). Without critical thinking, this is the first thing that comes to mind and then exits the mouth. The base thought is our real feelings (what is motivating the top thought and seems really vulnerable to say out loud). Most of the time when we talk with each other, we talk from our top thought, hoping to resolve our base thought or how we actually feel.

The problem with this way of communicating is that we are only sharing part of the message. Our real message is located in our base thought, the vulnerable gut feeling we are hoping to get across but are unaware of or too fearful to share. This can often be a root cause of conflict because we aren't talking about what is really going on. As a result, we dance around an issue with our top thoughts in hopes that somehow our partner will pick up on our base thoughts, magically understand us, and then do something to make the situation better. What usually happens is the opposite. Top thoughts often contain language that can be blaming, shaming, or critical; intellectual language that can be factual, data driven, and lacks emotion; or distorted language, using cloudy thinking like mistaken beliefs and assumptions about yourself, your partner, or your relationship. Using top thought communication like this often engages conflict and raises defensiveness.

Using our base thoughts works differently. Unlike top thoughts, when you talk from your base, you don't put up a front or ask your partner to decode your thoughts and feelings. Instead, your base exposes the actual concerns and emotions you have and makes space for your partner to really hear what is going on. Furthermore, speaking from your base thoughts rather than just your top thoughts or first reaction creates an opportunity for empathy. Hearing that your partner feels scared, sad, or discouraged typically invokes a sense of care, allowing your reactions to move from defensive to understanding. No one likes it when his or her partner blames them in anger or makes assumptions about circumstances. However, if you understand that the anger is there because your partner feels hurt or disappointed, or that assumptions are made because your partner is afraid of your reaction, understanding grows and conversations become collaborations.

Action

It is essential to remember that your partner cannot read your mind and doesn't know how you feel if you do not tell him or her. Our partners don't have an X-ray into base thoughts. It is our job to identify how we feel and what is motivating our reaction, or top thought. This can take some work, at first, especially for those who are big top talkers. Also, this is a more vulnerable way of communicating with each other.

It can be very helpful, and more successful, for you and your partner to read this chapter and practice using base thoughts together. Here is a Pre-Talk Thought technique you can use with any conversation:

1. Write down your answers to the following questions:

    a.   Pick a topic, something easy to start. Now, think about what you would naturally want to say and write that down. This is your top thought.

    b.   Next, ask yourself, "What is motivating what I am saying? What is the feeling(s) that is underneath my statement?" Try forming a statement using your base thoughts or feelings. A *Base-Thought Statement* might sound like this: "I am feeling (emotion words, like sad, disappointed, scared, worried, upset, frustrated, anxious, etc.) about (your concern)."

2. Now, engage in a conversation with your partner.

    a.   Let your partner know you have done some Pre-Talk Thinking and would like to try having a base-thought conversation. Ask if they are willing to do that with you.

    b.   Next, start the conversation by using the Base-Thought Statement you wrote above. Here is an example you can lead with: "Can we talk about (your concern)? I am feeling (your Base-Thought Statement from above) and need to talk it through with you."

3. As you and your partner try this with each other, it can be helpful to share both your top thought and your base thought with each other, examining the differences along with why you would choose not to share your base feeling with him or her.

Take turns throughout the conversation going back and forth.

    a.   Going forward, you can always check in with yourself before a conversation by asking, "What do I naturally want to say right now? Is that how I really feel, or is it what I feel safe saying?" This can offer great insight regarding the real conversation at hand.

    b.   As a couple, you can hold one another accountable by *kindly asking* each other, "Is that your top thought or base thought?" Often, you can change a conversation from a conflict to collaboration just by moving from your top thought to your base thought together.

{Reset Your Critical Thinking Skills}

MIND BENDER
Speaking from Your Gut

1. As you practiced using the Pre-Talk Thought exercise, what did you learn about yourself?

2. Was it easy or hard to identify your base thoughts? Why or why not?

3. Was it difficult to share how you felt with your partner? Why or why not?

4. When using your top thoughts and base thoughts in conversation with your partner, what insights did you have?

5. How did using your base thought change your conversation?

How Will Becoming More Critical Revolutionize Your Relationship?

Speaking from your base thoughts immediately helps your partner understand you better. It reveals the real feelings at play in your relationship. When you and your partner are having a base-to-base conversation, it speeds up your communication and expedites problem resolution. Having access to the motivations behind your conversations radically changes the level of empathy in the relationship and builds a deeper sense of intimacy.

11

Relational Accounting 101

Any CPA can tell you the importance of a ledger. A ledger is the simple system of recording credits and debits, like what you see when you open your bank statement or online bank account. It keeps track of all deposits and withdrawals, along with maintaining a running balance. By quickly looking at the balance, you know if things are going well or if there is a problem. When the ledger isn't balanced, there are outstanding debts, and someone is left responsible until the debts are paid.

Did you know that every family keeps a ledger too? Renowned Hungarian American psychiatrist Ivan Boszormenyi-Nagy documented this theoretical viewpoint in 1973 in his book *Invisible Loyalties*, helping to define the psychological power of family systems from one generation to the next. According to Boszormenyi-Nagy, transgenerational accounting or The Family Ledger is the intangible place where all relational and emotional transactions throughout the generations get recorded. This ledger also holds both assets and liabilities: actions, behaviors, values, and traits that either damaged or enhanced the family. These ledgers affect many aspects of our lives as couples as they provide our models for functional or dysfunctional relationships. Here's a simple example: If your parents modeled a loving and caring relationship, that would be an asset they send forward; but if your parents modeled a high conflict and complicated relationship, it would send forward a liability. Here's a more serious example: If your father was an alcoholic who was unavailable to the family because of his addiction, that would send forward a liability; but if your father was an alcoholic who went through treatment, recovered, and repaired his family relationships, that could balance the ledger and send forward an asset.

Every generation inherits the ledger created by the previous generations, and every new generation can carry forward the same assets and liabilities or positively balance the ledger by getting rid of liabilities for the next generation. When couples get together, they both bring their family ledgers with them, and together they have the opportunity and great responsibility of merging their books, resolving the liabilities, and holding on to the assets provided by two family systems. By doing so, couples create a new ledger and legacy for their relationship and for their immediate family, which they will send forward. From this perspective, couples have an incredible power to affect the next generation together. Paying attention and actively working toward building a life of assets will gain benefits not just in your relationship, but also for generations to come.

The key to balancing and rebalancing relational books is found in consciously utilizing the act of forgiveness. Holding on to old wounds leaves debts or liabilities on the ledger that will eventually need to be balanced. These can be hurts from previous generations that negatively affect your relationship or hurts that have been created in your current relationship. Old wounds are not productive in the present. Sometimes these are big hurts that remain unresolved, and sometimes they are little ways we dismiss each other or don't attend to the relationship. Four opportunities are waiting when it comes to applying forgiveness in your relationship:

1. *Resolving liabilities from previous generations.* Sometimes we inherit dysfunctional ways of relating because that was what our family modeled for us. Sometimes we carry forward old wounds that shut us down emotionally and make us unavailable to be the best partner possible. Forgiving your parents, role models, or previous generations for leaving you with a liability is important. By doing so, you are saying you no longer want that experience in your life and your relationship. You are going to be different. In your generation, you will resolve this debt and pay it off through forgiveness and change. It will end with you.

2. *Asking for forgiveness from your partner.* If you have caused your partner pain and never asked for forgiveness, don't delay any longer. You have a unique opportunity to make things right. By adopting the position of a Humble Warrior, you can make a major change in the ledger of your relationship by acknowledging the hurt you have caused, having remorse, and sharing with your partner what you have learned. This can change things going forward. Asking for forgiveness is a powerful act that can produce extraordinary results.

3. *Extending forgiveness to your partner.* Are you grasping on to a grudge in your relationship or harboring old wounds as ammunition for the future? Maybe it is time to try forgiveness. So often we confuse the process of forgiveness with the process of redemption. We think that we can only forgive when appropriate acknowledgment of wrongdoing or remorse is present in our partner and they show how they are making

up for their terrible behavior. Actually, one of the biggest advantages of forgiveness is that it only requires one person to make it happen: you. Holding on to hurt occupies your mind and heart, using time and energy that can be spent moving forward toward positive change.

4. *Forgiving yourself.* Shame is a wicked master that can keep you chained in self-deprecation and holding you to a half-life in your relationship. We all make mistakes in life. You will continue to suffer unnecessarily by refusing to let yourself off the hook after you have resolved a hurt in your relationship. In doing so, you rob both yourself and your partner of the best life you can have together.

Action

One of the greatest definitions of forgiveness I have ever heard came from a conversation between two passionate healers in the world of self-help, Oprah Winfrey and Tony Robbins. It has been transformative in my life and the lives of many clients as it makes a clear pathway for forgiveness to manifest. The definition is this: Forgiveness is a process of taking what has hurt you, or how you have hurt someone else, learning and changing from it, and then letting it go by saying, "Thank you *For Giving* me this lesson." Identifying what you have learned and how you can change from a painful experience releases you. Finding a way that the wounds or misgivings have contributed to your personal growth in relationship with yourself, others, and the world around you fills negative space with gratitude. By instigating this process, you let go of a liability and replace it with the asset of wisdom.

Pick an offense that you have been holding on to from a previous generation or in your relationship. Maybe it is the thing you bring up frequently and just can't let go of, the moment that still lingers as unresolved in your mind, the topic that makes you wince whenever it comes up in conversation, the circumstance that still boils your blood even though ten years have gone by. Or it might be the issue you avoid at every cost and just cross your fingers that your partner won't ever bring up. Whatever it is for you, take that issue through the following six-step process. It can be really helpful to write down your responses to each step:

1. *Examine the offense.* Take a long, hard look at what has happened to cause this hurt. In hindsight, what do you understand about the choices that were made and the circumstances that occurred?

2. *Define your growth.* What have you learned about yourself through this experience? What have you learned about your partner? What have you learned about your relationship? How can everything you learned help you and your partner have a better relationship in the future? Make a list of the changes you will make and how your relationship has changed as a result of this experience.

3. *Ask for forgiveness, if needed.* Through examination, how did you contribute to what happened? Were they your choices that inflicted harm? When hurt, did you react and hurt back? If needed, go to your partner with these three sentences: "I am sorry for ____. I was wrong. I hope, when you are ready, you will forgive me." That is it—no extra words, justifications, or backpedaling.

4. *Say thanks.* After all of this analysis, thank the circumstance for what it has taught you. Thank it for the wisdom it has offered and the changes it will bring. Thank it for the reminders it

leaves behind of how *not* to be in your relationship and for the guidance it provides for how to relate better with your partner.

5. *Let it go.* Once you can define your growth and thank the circumstance, it has served its purpose. Document it in your relationship book of learning, and close the chapter. Now, whenever your mind remembers this event, it will do so with sound reason and closure. It is no longer worthwhile to keep it in your hands and carry it with you.

6. *Release your issue.* As you complete this process, feel the weight lift off of you and your relationship. Both you and your partner will benefit greatly from taking the time to thoroughly process, grow, and learn from these burdens. Not only have you erased an old debt, but you have replaced it with the asset of learning how to love and care for one another even better than before. You may want to share your process with your partner, letting them in on how you have grown and what you have learned. You also may wish to keep this experience to yourself. The great thing about forgiveness is that it can happen independently and still bring about positive change.

{Reset Your Relational Ledger}

MIND BENDER
Thanks-for-Giving

After you have processed through your issue(s) above, reflect on the following:

What was the most difficult part of this process for you?

Is there anything left undone that you need support to complete?

What type of support do you need? Go get it!

○———————————————————————————○

How Will Thanks-for-Giving Revolutionize Your Relationship?

Forgiveness clears the air between you and your partner, making it easier to be together. Without old baggage and heavy burdens, your relationship will feel more positive and possible. Forgiveness is the path to a long-term, peaceful relationship, building a ledger of assets not just for your relationship and family, but also for generations yet to come.

12

Three Positives

Insight

Have you ever had the experience of buying a new car, and all of a sudden you see the same car everywhere? This occurs because of a place in your brain called the Reticular Activating System (RAS). It is the part of your primitive or mammalian brain that is responsible for multiple functions, including sleeping, waking, bodily functions, and consciousness. When you go under anesthesia during surgery, this is the part of your brain that is managed, keeping you comfortably unaware of your surroundings. It also operates the critical function of focus, working as a filter for the millions of pieces of data that we take in daily.

Without your RAS working properly, you would be overwhelmed, overstimulated, and unable to function well. One of the great properties of the RAS is its ability to modify focus based on the thoughts, feelings, and goals we assign to it. So, if we are trying to sort out a bowl of M&M's and only want to keep the red ones, it will help us to only see the red M&M's. Or, if you are specifically looking for a cucumber in the grocery store, you will zoom in on it when you hit the produce department. It also helps us focus on more important tasks. For example, if your goal is to save money, and then you find yourself feeling good when you look at your bank account, your RAS system registers this association and will help maintain focus on your goal. In like fashion, if you want to feel better about your partner, your RAS system is there to help. By making it a priority to look for the positives in your relationship and focusing on those experiences, your brain is going to home in on the good feelings that go along with them. In this case, you will find the "law of attraction" at work—the more you focus on something, the more you will experience it.

Action

In the 1990s, Dr. Martin Seligman spearheaded the breakthrough field of Positive Psychology. Although Abraham Maslow had used the term Positive Psychology years earlier, very little research had been done on why happy people were happy. In his book *Authentic Happiness*, Dr. Seligman explains how he spent years in the field and study of psychology with the usual approach to mental health problems. Typically, a client would come see a therapist, and together they would discuss all of the problems in the clients' life in hopes of resolving his or her concerns. After years of practicing this approach himself, Dr. Seligman wondered what might happen if instead of focusing on the negative in client's lives, clinicians started focusing on the positive. This simple question inspired a whole new division of psychology, which has proven what seems like an obvious conclusion—it makes people feel better to focus on the positives. The same applies for couples. When partners continually focus on their problems, the relationship suffers. However, when they shift their focus to the positive aspects of their relationship, the overall mood in the relationship rises. The following Three Positives exercise is so simple, and it is scientifically proven to lift the mood in your relationship. Working with your partner, commit to doing this every day for the next three weeks. Be committed and stick with it; I think you will love the results.

{Reset Your Focus}

○————————————————————————————————○

MIND BENDER
Three Positives

1. You will need to find a place to write down your positive thoughts, whether it is a notebook, a journal, a whiteboard, or a text thread. It is suggested that both you and your partner do this together, so keep what you are writing on in a place that is accessible for both of you—maybe in your bedroom, on your kitchen table, or on your smartphone.

2. *Every day* for the next three weeks, *each* of you will write down three positive things about each other and/or your relationship. They can be simple, such as "You smiled at me this morning," "You remembered my big meeting," or "When we were leaving, you kissed me goodbye." Or they can be more tangible, like "You washed my car," "You took me out for dinner," or "You made sure the bills were paid." They can be anything that feels positive. Be sure to read what your partner writes; it will feel good.

3. After three weeks, get together and review what you have written about the relationship and each other. How have you felt more positive about each other throughout these three weeks? Take turns telling your partner the positive ways this exercise has affected your relationship.

You don't have to stop doing this after three weeks! If it is working, I encourage you to keep it going. Can you imagine the uplifting book you will write together by the end of a year? Not to mention, imagine how grateful you will be for your partner. Now, that is good stuff.

How Will Three Positives Revolutionize Your Relationship?

As the two of you start to focus on the positive, you will begin to see more positives in the relationship. Fostering an attitude of gratitude is contagious and will affect each partner's overall mood in the relationship and in individual experiences. When the dominant feeling is positive, everything has greater possibility and the future looks bright.

13

CLEAN SLATE PROTOCOL

Insight

At the end of the blockbuster movie *Iron Man 3*, Tony Stark, the unflappable techno-entrepreneur, makes a bold decision for Pepper Potts, the woman he loves. He takes the one thing that has continually been a problem in their relationship (the Iron Man Project), and in a moment, he blows it all up, running what he refers to as the Clean Slate Protocol. After years of his career coming first before their relationship, he realizes that the only way for the relationship to succeed is for him to readjust his priorities. This is a common occurrence in many couple relationships. As the years go by, everything from valid pursuits to unproductive vices weasel their way into top position for our time and attention. This leaves the relationship and our partner feeling unimportant and disconnected.

What is so great about the scene in *Iron Man 3* is the dramatic exaggeration of such a simple choice. If your relationship is important, then this choice is easy—just blow up whatever is standing in the way. You can choose to do this for your relationship. Is there an issue or concern that is at the center of the discontent and conflict between you and your partner? Maybe it is extra time spent at the office, volunteering, or on a hobby that takes priority over your relationship. It could be outside relationships, whether with family or friends, that you put in front of your partner. And often it can be our own vices, such as social networking, online gaming, alcohol use, overspending, overeating, or overexercising that consume our thoughts and time, keeping us distracted from what matters most. Whatever it is, run the Clean Slate Protocol, and get rid of this concern. It is just a choice, and you can make it at any time for the benefit of the relationship you claim is most important in your life. Do it now—before it is too late.

Action

First, write your *own* Clean Slate Declaration. A declaration is an announcement that recognizes the authority and truth in something important. You can only write this proclamation personally, for yourself. You cannot write this for your partner and give it to them.

This is simple and can look like this:

I am running the Clean Slate Protocol on _____
(concern in our relationship), and as of _____
(time) I will no longer be doing _____.
BOOM!

Now, follow through with that plan by using the following suggestions:

- You might need to destroy something to reduce the temptation to revert back—do it! Freeze a credit card, empty the liquor cabinet, delete social networking sites, turn off your phone, etc.

- You might need to set new boundaries and reallocate your

time—do it! Reset expectations with family, cut down the frequency of nights out, limit the time you have available for work outside of office hours, etc.

•   You might need to get help if you are worried that it is going to be hard—do it! Get some accountability, a support team that you can go to when it gets tough. That can include your partner, positive friends, or an organized program or support group. Go to counseling if your vices have too much control over your life.

•   If you run the Clean Slate Protocol, be mindful that you're doing it with an open heart and that it's your choice. Resentment about making the decision will build animosity. Giving something up as a Loving Observer allows you to release because the choice was yours to make, and you made it with an open heart.

{Reset Your Reality}

MIND BENDER

Clean Slate Declaration

After writing your Clean Slate Declaration:

1. Announce your Clean Slate Declaration to your partner. Have a conversation about your decision. Talk about the support you need from your partner and any outside resources, like a counselor, doctor, or organized program.

2. Next, post a copy of the declaration on your bathroom mirror or somewhere you will see it daily as a reminder of your commitment.

3. Set celebration points where you and your partner can mark the time that has passed since the Clean Slate Declaration was first made. It usually takes focused time and rewards to change a behavior. Put a plan in place to help you succeed. If you miss or slip up, please don't give up! Just blow it up and start again.

How Will the Clean Slate Protocol Revolutionize Your Relationship?

Actions speak so much louder than words. Showing your partner what you are willing to do for the relationship is a game changer. Making dramatic decisions to benefit the relationship solidifies your commitment and brings couples closer together. Prioritizing your relationship is a radical action that produces positive long-term results.

MUSCLE BUILDERS
Create a Strong Connection

Muscle Builders are exercises that challenge you as a couple to find new ways to connect and, in turn, increase the strength of your relationship. Everything in our life that we desire to have longevity and sustainability requires strength. If you want your body to last, you need good eating and exercise habits. If you want financial security, you need good saving habits. If you want to succeed in your career, you need to work hard. Great couple relationships are the same way. If you want them to go the distance, together you both need to put some muscle into it!

INSIGHT + ACTION + PRACTICE = POSTIVE CHANGE

14

The Epic Kiss

Insight

Casablanca, *Spider-Man*, *Titanic*, and *The Notebook*—all of these movies have one thing in common: an Epic Kiss! Not only do they each have these moments where the characters fall into each other's arms and lock lips, but each of the kisses lasts at least six seconds. If you know anything about the film industry, you know that every second counts, and when the time is given to a scene it is because it really matters. What if I told you that time really matters when you kiss your partner too? There is actually truth to the fact that if you kiss your partner for six seconds or longer, you create a more intimate connection. Dr. John Gottman, who has studied couple relationships for decades, confirms that the six-second kiss is a key to couple happiness. Through this small act of time, you will enable a big act of intimacy that your relationship needs. Think about it: When was the last time you really kissed your partner? You know what I am talking about: the kind of kisses that you couldn't get enough of when you first met, the kind of kisses where, if someone saw you, their reaction would be "Get a room!" Those are your Epic

Kisses. They belong to your relationship, and they need to continue to show up throughout the length of your relationship to give strength and stability to your intimacy.

Action

So, let's practice your Epic Kiss. Initially, you may be surprised at how long six seconds actually is. First, set a stopwatch and just kiss, stopping when it feels long enough. You may find that only two to three seconds have gone by. This is a common occurrence. Maybe you made it to six seconds or beyond—good for you! Now, set a timer for six seconds and lay one on each other again. Let this one be a true Epic Kiss, where the world falls away and time stands still. Really get into this kiss until the timer goes off. (If it is so great, you don't have to stop!) Note how different it feels to be with each other with that much intention and time given to the task. Do you feel the increased connection? Do you feel time stand still for a moment? What a phenomenal gift to have an Epic Kiss with your partner! Now, try this for the next thirty days: Every time you leave each other and every time you reunite, give each other (at minimum) a six-second kiss. There is *always* an extra six seconds to give to your partner twice a day, so no "I am too busy" excuses. Maybe you even want to have a healthy competition and try to never be the first one to stop. After all, Hollywood shouldn't own the Epic Kiss—you should!

{Reset Your Connection}

MUSCLE BUILDER
Your Epic Kiss

1. Establish your Epic Kiss.

2. Practice your Epic Kiss twice a day for thirty days.

3. Make a daily Epic Kiss a part of your Relationship Revolution.

Have someone take a picture of your Epic Kiss and put it somewhere you see every day: on your screen saver, on a wall in your home, on your desk, or wherever you like.

How Will the Epic Kiss Revolutionize Your Relationship?

The Epic Kiss reengages your intimacy daily, creating a vital connection to keep your relationship strong. When you make an intention to intimately connect daily, it increases your attention on each other, creating a renewed desire for one another. Own your Epic Kiss. Move beyond thirty days, and add this to your relationship lifestyle. Make every day your romance, your love story, your movie moment.

15

"Can You Hear Me?"

Insight

You know that tone. The one your partner uses when they need something from you, when they are disappointed, or when they are feeling frisky. As a matter of fact, you often don't even register the words they use. The tone is enough to instigate an emotional reaction. And then there is the body language—the arms across the chest, the disappointed look, or the move in for a hug. In our relationships, much of of our communication happens nonverbally. Communication scholars suggest it is somewhere between 60 to 90 percent, and we are well-attuned to the messages that this nonverbal energy brings.

Scientists out of the HeartMath Institute have been studying the intuitive connection between communication and heart reactions for years. One outstanding fact they have uncovered is that the human heart has a built-in sensory system that feels what is coming before the head even registers what is happening. Our bodies read each other efficiently and quickly in our communication, even when words aren't present. When the message does reach the head, our brains are also helping us to understand each other even when the information is limited. A current study in *The Journal of Neuroscience* is showing how our brains work as predictive machines in conversation. As partners communicate with each other, their brain patterns begin to mirror one another, resulting in an increased anticipation of what is going to be said. This may be the reason we can understand what our partner means even when they can't find the words and could potentially be the cause of being able to finish each other's sentences!

Over time, as we learn how our partner thinks and reacts in a long-term, committed relationship, couples develop what can be referred to as Predictive Listening. Predictive Listening is the ability to decipher messages and meaning in an accurate and efficient manner before all of the information is communicated. Between the intuitive skills of the heart and prognostic capacity of the brain, Predictive Listening benefits the relationship by speeding up our communication, formulating our connections, and increasing our relational intelligence with one another.

However, a drawback occurs when our predictions are inaccurate. The movement from Predictive Listening to making Predictive Assumptions is frequently at the root of miscommunication. Miscommunication happens when one person applies meaning to a message that the other person didn't intend to communicate. Hallmark responses to a miscommunication include phrases like "I didn't hear you say that," or "I thought you meant . . ." This creates frustration in a relationship and problems that could have been avoided if couples had checked in on what was being communicated rather than assuming meaning that wasn't accurate.

Action

One of the simplest and most rudimentary interpersonal communication tools is called a Shared Meaning. A Shared Meaning occurs by *slowing down* and *breaking down* our dialogue with one another, checking in on the actual meaning behind the words that are spoken. What I love about going back to the basics of our communication is how quickly and effectively the tools can be implemented and result in positive change.

Initially, learning the basics of communication is like riding a bike. For most people, learning how to ride a bike feels a bit awkward. Maybe you remember what it felt like when you first learned. At first, you are aware of everything, from your feet on the pedals, to your hands on the handlebars, to where the brakes are, to which way you need to turn. And on top of all that is the death-defying feeling of being off-balance. Every detail is top of mind, and riding feels cumbersome. Then, after riding awkwardly for a while, all of the pieces come together, and before you know it, all you are thinking about is how fast you can go or what a beautiful day it is.

Breaking down your communication with the following Shared Meaning exercise can feel very similar. It might seem goofy to talk so simply with your partner, but as you practice it over and over again, you will eventually get good at it. Once this happens, you will find that your communication is easier and has more clarity. Then when you do have moments of miscommunication in your relationship, you have a go-to tool to help you out!

{Reset Your Communication}

MUSCLE BUILDER
Shared Meaning Exercise

This simple exercise can be used to clarify any conversation. It allows the listener to confirm what's been heard and the speaker to bring clarity to what they are attempting to communicate. Here is an example of how to use this technique:

> Partner 1 makes a statement: "I would really like to go out for dinner on Saturday."

> Partner 2 responds with, "What I hear you saying is . . ." and then repeats what they heard: "You want to go out for dinner on Saturday night so we don't have to cook." (Notice that Partner 2 took the liberty to add in an assumption.)

> Partner 1 either confirms the meaning by saying, "Yes, that is what I said," or clarifies by saying, "No, that isn't what I said."

> In this case, Partner 1 would say, "No, that isn't what I said. What I said was . . ."

> Next, Partner 1 repeats their original statement, modifying it as needed: "I would really like to go out for dinner on Saturday night because it would be fun."

> Partner 2 then tries again and responds with, "What I hear you saying is . . ." and then repeats *only* what he or she heard: "You would really like to go out for dinner on Saturday night because it would be fun."

> Partner 1 responds with, "Yes—that is what I said, and that is what I meant."

You repeat this process as many times as necessary to make sure that what the speaker is saying and what the listener is hearing are the same thing. Here are a couple tips to keep in mind:

- *Stop assuming.* It can be very easy to attribute meaning to our partner's words and, in turn, add in information that he or she is not communicating. When this happens, it gives you a chance to clarify if your assumption is accurate or not.

- *Nonverbals matter.* Sometimes how a partner says something does have more meaning than the words he or she uses. At that point, it is important for the speaking partner to modify their tone or body language so that his or her verbal and nonverbal communications match. This helps prevent miscommunication going forward.

How Will "Can You Hear Me?" Revolutionize Your Relationship?

Slowing down and breaking down your communication allows for better connection and clarity. The more you feel heard and understood, the better you will feel about each other. Knowing how to clarify in the moment is a critical skill to prevent long-term problems and build effective communication for a lifetime.

16

Let's Get It On

Insight

Thank you, Marvin Gaye. What would a couples-relationship book be without talking about getting it on? Incomplete, to say the least, for it is sex that delineates a romantic relationship from a friendship. What sets committed couple relationships apart is the fact that we get naked with each other—one of the most intimate and vulnerable human states of being. Next to money, sex is one of the hardest topics for most adults to discuss, and it frequently causes frustration in the relationship.

For most people, the only time they get formal sex education is in middle school or high school, while the rest is often learned through experience. This experience comes from a variety of places, which can include personal sexual history (family of origin, religion, sexual development, and sexual experiences); past sexual partners (both positive and negative); media-delivered sexual messages (often containing unrealistic expectations, objectification, body-image standards, and a range of pornographic images that don't fit in reality); current sexual expression and partners; and fantasies of possible sexual expression. When a couple gets together, they bring all of this history and education, accurate or not, with them to the bedroom. And we wonder why couple's sex lives get complicated.

Yet sex is thrilling, intensely pleasurable, and chemically reactive. If your relationship were a brick wall, the bricks would be the pieces of your lives stacked upon each other, while sex would be the mortar in between holding it all together. Sex is a bonding agent. It is not only emotionally bonding but also physiologically bonding as it creates a hormonal cocktail of dopamine, oxytocin, and vasopressin. Dopamine is like cocaine to the brain, lighting up the pleasure center; oxytocin occurs through orgasm and creates attachment; and vasopressin is produced after sex and is attributed to sustaining commitment. Together they create a vitamin supplement for a long-term relationship.

Action

Now don't freak out, but sex changes throughout the course of a lifelong relationship. But I bet you already knew that. It's just that most couples silently suffer in their sex life, blaming each other for sex not being everything they hoped for or wanted, when changes in a couple's sex life are actually perfectly normal. Here are a few things every couple needs to know about sex in a long-term, monogamous relationship:

- *It's OK.* Sex usually slows down after the initial attraction phase, which typically lasts around six to eighteen months. Couples may see the intensity of their sexual connection start to fade, and it is so important to understand that this is a common occurrence and not a sign that this is the "wrong" relationship. Talking about these changes can be really helpful along with building an understanding of each other's desire for frequency of intimacy, what constitutes rejection for each partner, and the importance of both partners initiating sex. Not discussing this experience can build unintended walls between partners from feeling rejected or unwanted.

• *Keep focused.* A couple's sex life can take a hit as the relationship takes on more responsibilities and distractions, particularly in the We/I Plateau. During these years, intentionally tending to your sexual connection is as important as taking care of your bodies or paying your bills. If you let it slide, there are natural consequences of loss of connection and attraction that follow. So stay focused on each other, and make time for sex.

• *Let go.* Expectations for how sex is "supposed to be" can get in the way. Sometimes sex is physical, sometimes it is emotional, sometimes it is spiritual, and sometimes it is a mixture. Sometimes it is great, and sometimes it is functional. Sometimes it is erotic, and sometimes it is typical. The best things you can do are release judgment and enjoy each other in the moment, whatever that moment brings.

• *Be patient.* There can be physical reasons that couples may need to delay or refrain from having sex, such as pregnancy, illness, surgery, or mental health concerns. In these circumstances, it is important that couples are talking about the fact that their sexual relationship is on hold and discussing if there are other intimate ways they can maintain a bond during these periods.

• *Don't give up.* Couples may find throughout the course of a lifetime together that they encounter sexual difficulties. These can include lack of desire and/or misaligned desire; problems with arousal, erection, and orgasm; or unresolved negative sexual experiences or traumas that need attention. Often due to frustration and embarrassment, couples let these concerns linger. If you have any of these concerns, it is OK; you're not alone. The best thing you can do for yourself and your relationship is get support. See a doctor or a sex therapist if things aren't working right or if there are blocks in your sexual expression. You can find a good sex therapist through www.aasect.org.

- *Keep fit.* How you feel in your own skin and your physical health directly affect the quality of your sex life. As people's bodies change through pregnancy, weight gain, aging, and physical challenges, self-esteem can also shift to the negative. This can reduce how sexy you may feel and even create embarrassment to be naked with your partner. The very best way to combat this experience is to pursue a healthy lifestyle through diet and exercise. The healthier you feel, the more confident you feel. Furthermore, studies show that couples that commit to a healthy lifestyle together enjoy a deeper bond and greater long-term success. It isn't always easy, but it sure is worth it.

- *Lighten up.* More than anything, sex is supposed to be fun! Having a playful attitude about intimacy is a great way to relax with each other and increase desire. Sometimes a history of sexual stress turns the bedroom into a serious zone. Help it return to a place where you can just kick back with each other by taking a look at the following tips.

Ten Ideas to Make Better Love

1. *Get some sex education.* Explore books and websites, or take a field trip to an intimacy shop.

2. *Turn it up.* Increasing frequency leads to increased desire and attraction. Try having sex more often than you do currently. Maybe even get crazy and have sex every day for a defined period of time.

3. *Intimacy stands for "In to me see."* Let your partner in, and talk about what you are thinking and feeling, especially while you are together sexually.

4. *Avoid bedroom boredom.* "Do it" differently, and get out of the rut of a typical experience. Shift positions or locations, or share your sexual fantasies with each other and give them a try.

5. *Absence makes the heart grow fonder.* Try a short period of abstaining from sex while simultaneously talking about how great it is going to be when you have sex and what you want to do with each other.

6. *Slow it down to turn it up.* Use a sensate focus exercise by taking turns just touching each other with no expectations that you will have intercourse. Tell each other where you like to be touched and how.

7. *Set a play date.* Role-play with each other, acting out scenarios that turn you on, or play games like strip poker or pool, truth or dare, or twenty sex questions.

8. *Be the teacher.* Pay attention to your own body and give your partner a lesson in what you like, how you want to be touched, and what is enjoyable for you.

9. *Get back to the basics.* Have a naked day. Get your house to yourself or get away and spend the day together au naturel.

10. *Free your mind.* Be creative and keep it interesting by staying open to new ideas. When your partner suggests something new, as long as you're comfortable, don't shut him or her down—give it a try!

The biggest gift you and your partner can give to your sex life is positive, nonjudgmental attention. Take the time and go to school with each other, creating your personalized version of sex ed. Use the dialogue exercise that follows as your first lesson, and be sure to do your homework.

{Reset Your Sex Life}

MUSCLE BUILDER
Couples Sex Ed

Get together with your partner and talk through the following questions:

1. What do we like about our sex life together? What works well? What do we enjoy?

2. How could we make our sex life together better?

3. Do either of us have concerns about our sex life together that need to be addressed? If so, what is the plan to take care of these concerns?

Now, pick out three items off the Ten Idea list that you want to implement into your sex life, and decide when you are going to do it!

How Will "Let's Get It On" Revolutionize Your Relationship?

Exploring your intimacy and sex life together can instantly reconnect you and your partner. Talking about sex and trying new ways of being together sexually ignites your relationship. Prioritizing an ongoing exploration of your sexual connection will intensify the bonds that keep you together and satisfied for a lifetime.

17

Vision Quest

Insight

There is a biblical Proverb that says, "Where there is no vision, the people perish" (Prov. 19:18). Nowhere is this more evident than in a couple's relationship that is stuck in a rut. Nine times out of ten a stuck couple lacks a shared vision, and without a shared vision, it is hard to stay focused and engaged in the relationship. Do you have a collective vision of why you are together and what you want to accomplish in this one beautiful life you have with each other? David Bach, a financial advisor and author of many books, including *Smart Couples Finish Rich*, has a fantastic model that he uses when helping couples formulate their financial planning goals. It is called a Values Circle™. I really like what David offers, particularly his holistic view of couples' financial health and his personal generosity. He actually offers his concept and chapter on financial values for free on his website, FinishRich.com. This is a resource I commonly refer couples to, but not just for financial planning.

The value of the Value Circle™ is its application for all aspects of a couple's relationship, because it is our values that motivate our actions. We spend our time, money, attention, and energy on what we value most. And just like how couples may approach conflict from different perspectives, couples often value different things in life. These differences in values, in turn, can cause couples to desire to put their time, money, attention, and energy in different places. And when values aren't lining up, couples feel misaligned and out of sync. This causes frustration, because working on any project from different angles makes it difficult to achieve a common purpose.

Any company worth its salt knows that alignment of values and purpose is critical to success, which is why they write a mission or vision statement. This statement is a guidepost that includes important values and goals that lead to a desired outcome. It has enormous power to light the path and show what matters day to day as they strive to achieve a greater long-term goal. For couples, identifying the important values they each hold, defining their purposes for being together, and creating a shared vision statement can help decrease common frustrations that arise around finances, leisure time, social circles, family priorities, community involvement, spiritual experiences, educational goals, health and fitness, and even sex and intimacy. All of these areas have one thing in common: They are thrown off course when couples fall out of alignment.

Action

First, let's define a value. A value is something that is important to you in life and reflects what you want in the world. It defines what really matters to you. Here are a few examples of values:

Adventure	Faith	Love
Balance	Family	Loyalty
Community	Freedom	Peace
Compassion	Friends	Power
Connectedness	Generosity	Security
Enlightenment	Growth	Spirituality
Excitement	Health	Stability
Experience	Independence	

Values are the drivers behind your desired goals or accomplishments in life, the pursuits that offer you purpose. As a couple, you likely share some values. Often our shared values are what attract us to one another and, in turn, keep us together. However, you will also find that each of you may hold equally important differing values that need to be considered. For example, think about what may occur in a couple if one partner values freedom and the other partner values security. Both of these are important values. However, if they aren't discussed, each partner may be pursuing those values in ways that contradict one another. One partner may pursue freedom by looking to take as many vacation days as possible, while the other partner pursues security by working extra hours as often as possible to save more money or have job stability. Without understanding what is motivating these opposite actions, this couple would most likely be at odds with each other. Can you hear the fights? "Why are you working so much!" versus "Why are you taking so much time off!" Talking through each of your top values is critical to have clarity behind what is motivating to one another and driving daily decisions. Also, discussing values is a conversation that needs to happen again and again over the years as values can change over time.

Next, let's take a look at purpose. Purpose defines your reasons for being together or why you exist as a couple. Do you know what your shared purposes are as a couple? There can be many different purposes for couples; here are a handful of ideas:

Create a business	Build a family	Travel the world
Enjoy companionship	Experience intimacy	Support others
Fulfill dreams	Leave a legacy	Give generously
Educate others	Love and be loved	
	Make a difference	

You will have multiple purposes in being together, and these too may change over time. Likewise, there may be one or two overarching purposes that will go the distance of the relationship. Just like your values, understanding your shared purpose is necessary to enhance your experience with each other. Then, beyond understanding, shared purpose defines the goals you want to accomplish in your life together. This provides direction for your relationship, giving vision to why it exists and what it is striving toward both daily and long term.

Finally, let's define vision. Vision is the projection of a desired outcome, a dream of possibility in the future. Visions fill us with hope and give meaning to our actions. For example, we go to work motivated by the vision of a paycheck that is coming after the work is done. Or we build a house step by step because there is a vision of what it will be like when it is completed. Visions are motivational and are typically positive and rewarding results from actions in the present. They are ultimately the drivers behind why we get up in the morning and what we accomplish in life. Without them, we experience depression and apathy coupled with a lack of direction.

We all need visions to express our purpose and feel valuable. Couples that have well-defined visions know what their life goals are, where they are headed, and why they are together.

Once you have explored your values and have examined your shared purposes, you are ready to build a vision statement for your relationship. It is possible you have worked on a vision statement before or maybe this is brand new to you. Following is a simple format that makes building a vision statement fairly easy. You may want to consider getting away and having a Vision Quest. This can be a day off you spend at home or a designated time away that is focused on clarifying your relationship and building your vision together for the future. Once you have written your vision statement, post it somewhere you can both see it every day.

{Reset Your Vision}

MUSCLE BUILDER
Build a Relationship Vision Statement

Values + Purposes = Vision

Answer the following questions:

1. *Define your values.* What values are important to you as a couple? What motivates what you do? Look back at the examples if you need some help.

2. *Define your purposes.* What are the reasons that you are together? What are your goals? Again, look back at the examples if you need to.

3. *Define your vision.* By examining your values and purposes, why does your relationship exist? When your lifetime is done, what do you hope your

children, family, friends, and the world remember about you as a couple?

Now, put those answers together in a Relationship Vision Statement: (add your words above to the parenthesis below).

Together, in the pursuit of (write in your shared values) with the desire to accomplish (write in your shared purposes), our relationship will aspire to (write in your shared vision).

Here is an example:

Together, in the pursuit of (VALUES: *love, education, and freedom*) with the desire to create (PURPOSES: *a loving family and make a difference in the world*), our relationship will aspire to (VISION: *always leave people and places better than we found them*).

How Will a Vision Quest Revolutionize Your Relationship?

Building a compelling shared vision breathes new life into your relationship. By activating critical conversations about your values and purposes, you will be reminded of the important things you hold in common. A focused direction for the future offers your relationship guidelines for how you spend your joint resources of time and money. Once a couple has a defined vision, they can step into a power alignment that not only changes their relationship, but can also change the world.

18

Say a Little Prayer for Me

Insight

Pierre Teilhard de Chardin was a French philosopher and Jesuit priest who contributed significantly to the study of evolution through the paleontological discovery of one of the oldest human skeletons, the Peking Man. In the midst of his scientific accomplishments, he developed an understanding that who we are spiritually supersedes who we are as human beings. As a result, one of Chardin's commonly attributed quotes is, "We are not human beings having a spiritual experience; we are spiritual beings having a human experience." From that vantage point, the couple relationship elevates into a realm that moves past our mortal comprehension. If you and your partner are two spiritual beings having a human love experience, then your access to support for your relationship extends far beyond the confines of earth.

A growing body of cutting-edge research on couples and religion reveals that when couples discuss and participate in a spiritual life together, genuine and lasting change can occur in the relationship. A recent study from the *Journal of Family Psychology* looked at over one thousand couples that professed a shared Christian faith. In those couples that activated their beliefs by praying together, the researchers found an increase in commitment and longevity in their relationships. Furthermore, by discussing their big faith questions with each other, including their doubts, joys, and fears, their bonds of intimacy were strengthened even if their beliefs were different. This highlights the value of integrating an active faith dialogue into our relationships.

Beyond a dialogue, ongoing research from the Institute of Noetic Sciences, a scientific community committed to the study of the fundamental powers and potential of consciousness, is digging into the effects of distant prayer between long-term committed couples on physical healing. The outcomes are surprisingly positive and worthy of a second look. The "Love Study" brought together couples in which one partner was fighting cancer. The healthy partner was taught how to meditate and focus on healing, loving intentions for their partner. Then, in a highly controlled research environment, the couples were separated and then measured for bodily reactions in response to the intentions of the trained partner. The results were astonishing. The sick partner's body responded time and again to the unknown healing intentions being sent by their partner, showing the powerful connection that exists beyond a couple's physical interaction.

In similar fashion, multiple university studies on the brain and the practice of meditation highlight the widespread impacts of this spiritual practice. The work of Sara Lazar, a neuroscientist at Massachusetts General Hospital and Harvard Medical School, has shown not only the significant results of meditation on everything from positive mood regulation to increased immune systems, but also documents meditation effecting the actual physical restructuring of the brain. Clearly prayer isn't a crutch, nor is it just for the religious.

Prayer is a vital way of connecting our spirits and bodies here on earth. We might say that prayer alone could have the power to revolutionize your relationship. There is power when two people come together in prayer, whether you choose to set intentions, meditate, or pray in traditional ways with each other. Do this in your relationship and watch out—there will be positive results!

Action

It really can't hurt you to try praying together. Just like stepping out and trying all of the other suggestions in this book, I encourage you to take a risk and pray with each other in one of the following ways:

- Praying together can be simple, such as choosing to meditate on the same quote, scripture verse, or positive intention for the relationship at the same time.

- Praying together can be traditional, using a prayer from your particular faith background and saying it out loud together.

- Praying together can be improvisational, each of you taking turns speaking out loud your desires and hopes for each other and your relationship.

- Praying together can be written, keeping a shared prayer journal where you write down your prayers for one another and your relationship.

There are many ways you can move your hearts and souls into spiritual alignment through multiple expressions of prayer. Try the following exercise with each other:

1. *Talk through the idea of praying together.* Before you step into this experience, discuss with your partnetr what feels comfortable. How have you personally used prayer, individually or jointly, before this exercise?

2. Pick one of the suggested ideas above, or make up your own way to pray together. Chose one way to pray together, and then decide how you want to proceed based on the idea you chose.

3. Dedicate a specific time. For this exercise to work, you need to give it some time. Pick a ten to fifteen minute time frame daily for the next three weeks. Maybe it works best to do this in the morning before the day takes off, or let this be your pillow talk before falling asleep.

4. Enjoy connecting on a spiritual level. Keep track of your experience and results. How has your time in prayer affected your relationship? Reflect on this below.

{Reset Your Spirits}

MUSCLE BUILDER
Creating a Spiritual Connection

Explain, if you can, your dedicated prayer experience.

Create a prayer plan with each other going forward. If you already have one, what is it?

Lay out how you can stay connected in prayer on a daily basis.

How are you supporting each other's spiritual journey currently, and what else could you do to support one another further?

How Will "Say a Little Prayer for Me" Revolutionize Your Relationship?

Joining together in prayer connects your relationship on a much deeper level. Experiencing the bonding outcome of prayer in your relationship will help both of you offer spiritual care for one another and the relationship. The long-term effects of prayer in your relationship will create a focus and loyalty to one another that is beyond your physical, emotional, and earthly experience.

19

Getting the Whole Picture

Insight

According to the great Merriam-Webster Dictionary, the soul can be defined as the immaterial essence, animating principle, or actuating cause of an individual life. So, if that is the case, our soul is the most critical part of who we are as human beings. Your soul is the essence of who you are—it is what makes you *you*. It is the very part that established your human-being-ness and, according to most religious traditions, the part that will remain for eternity. This also means that your partner's soul existed in fullness before you and will exist in fullness after you. So when you committed to a lifetime together, knowingly or not, you signed up to be the stewards of each other's soul. This is no small task. It requires you to see in your partner something deeper and genuinely care about his or her development and well-being on earth. Who does your partner need to become? What is your partner's purpose in the world? How can you help him or her get there? This is a practice in the continual growth of your compassion and kindness for each other.

Did you know that compassion and kindness are traits that can be cultivated? Stanford University research out of the Compassion Cultivation Training program confirms that these emotional muscles can grow stronger in people if they practice being in kind and compassionate states of mind. Not only does increased kindness and compassion contribute to greater functionality and satisfaction in long-term, committed relationships, but it also increases personal happiness. There is nothing more selfless than believing without a shadow of a doubt that you are here to help, encourage, and support your partner to become all he or she was meant to be in this world. After all, if being together doesn't allow that to manifest, you are actually getting in the way of the purpose of another soul. That sounds dangerous, doesn't it?

Action

This action will help you increase compassion and kindness for your partner while you explore the essence of who he or she is in life. It is best to have this experience simultaneously with your partner. Before you start, you will need to collect a childhood picture of your partner around the age of three to four years old (or as young as possible)—the cuter, the better. Once you have the photo, find a place to sit with the picture where you won't be interrupted and you can reflect for a while. Also, please turn off or let go of any distractions for the full duration of this exercise. Then settle into your place, and once you are ready, follow the reflection steps below:

Reflection 1

Take a moment and just look at the photo of your partner. Try to really see this little person. Everything you love about the depth of your partner's essence and personality is in this picture. It is known that our personality is well developed by the time we end our preschool years. How we act in the world is established early on in life and continues until we die. Although your impact on your partner is undeniable, it doesn't make him or her more real or validated as a person. Often we forget that the person we are with really matters to the world. They are here for a reason, just like you are. And that reason isn't to make you happy or fulfill your desires. Their soul has significance. We tend to acknowledge this fact when we are with little children and believe in the future that they will create. I want you to believe in your partner this way *today*. See your partner outside of the relationship, affirm his or her importance in the world, and love the essence of who he or she was, is, and always will be. As you look at this photo, acknowledge your partner for the unique and valuable soul he or she is in the world.

PAUSE—BREATHE—NEXT

Reflection 2

Now, think of this little person as the partner you love today. What similarity do you see in him or her as you compare the past to the present? Is it in their smile or eyes, the way his or her hair curls or cowlicks, or how he or she sits or stands? What do you know about that time in your partner's life? Is there any relevant information that defined your partner early on? What were his or her earliest hopes and dreams? What did your partner want to be when he or she grew up? These can be paramount pieces of who a person is and needs to become in the world. Are there ways that your partner has fulfilled his or her purpose that you can acknowledge and be proud of? Sometimes life takes us on unanticipated detours and old dreams lay dormant. Are there things your partner has yet to do that you can be supportive of?

PAUSE—BREATHE—NEXT

Reflection 3

Looking at this picture, has life changed your partner? Was there a sparkle in the eye of that child that is missing today? Life has a way of laying burdens on each of us as we grow up, often burying some essential pieces of our essence. Is there any way you can help your partner reconnect with aspects of himself or herself that have long been forgotten? Even as adults, the power of play can be a critical way of connecting with the child in us who still wants to laugh and be carefree. Ask your partner what he or she may need in order to tap into his or her playful side. Sometimes our childhoods were tough. Is there a part of your partner's history that needs healing? Can you be there for your partner and support his or her path to healing?

PAUSE—BREATHE—NEXT

Reflection 4

Finally, as you look at this little person, imagine yourself as a loving adult in their world. Can you see your partner at his or her full potential? Can you hold hopes and dreams for your partner and believe in his or her best future? Now—look at your partner. Holding this experience, try to see this little person in the adult that you love. Feel for your partner the love and care that you felt for his or her little version in the photo. Feel the importance of who your partner is in the world. Experience the reverence of your partner's unique and necessary purpose. Stand today as a steward of his or her soul.

PAUSE—BREATHE—NEXT

After you complete the action steps above, get together with your partner. Give them a big hug filled with the appreciation you have gained for their soul. Now, have the following conversation with your partner, taking turns sharing each other's experience:

{Reset Your Souls}

o——————————————————————o

MUSCLE BUILDER
Soul Stewards

The definition of being a steward is one that takes care of something that is of great value to another person. To be the steward of our partner's soul is to join them in caring for the essence of who they are and their purpose in the world—which is of great value to them.

1. Tell your partner what each of the reflection steps were like for you as you looked at his or her picture.

2. Ask your partner the following:

   What did you want to be when you were little? Has that changed, or is it still the same?

   What is left for you to do with your dreams, and how can I help you?

3. Ask your partner how you can be supportive as a steward of his or her soul.

o——————————————————————o

How Will Getting the Whole Picture Revolutionize Your Relationship?

Focusing on your partner as a soul that is bigger than the person you are in a relationship with builds respect for who your partner is and why he or she is in the world. This can be especially important in the daily moments—can you believe this eternal soul is choosing to make you dinner, do your laundry, or mow your lawn? Reverence for the eternal essence of who the other is puts into perspective the important pact you made together when you decided to commit for a lifetime. If you are going to remain happily together, you need to lift each other up to your best lives possible.

20

Keep It Interesting

Insight

At the end of every *Vanity Fair* magazine issue is a Proust questionnaire. This is a series of interview questions that are filled out by some notable, interesting, and often famous human being. The fun thing about the interview is that it allows for a sneak peek into the depths of someone's beliefs and character. Although the answers can be enlightening, humorous, and even profound at times, it is the origins of this questionnaire that are most intriguing for couples.

The questionnaire is associated with the French novelist Marcel Proust, who completed a similar set of questions back in the late 1800s, and due to his fame, the copy was preserved and curated throughout the years. The questions he answered were commonly found in something called a confession book. These books were placed in English homes during the nineteenth century, much like a guest book, to record visitors. The interesting purpose, however, was that the questions served to help couples get to know one another through the courting process. They were inquisitions into the character of an individual, revealing simple favorites to philosophical ideals. This was considered a fun game of "get to know you better," allowing couples to deepen their relationships during a modest period in which private, open dialogue between the sexes was frowned upon.

Of course, in today's world, this is no longer an issue at all. With the vast amount of information that can be accessed by someone online, to the myriad of ways people can communicate in private, to the extensive assessments and questionnaires used in online dating, we can know someone's personal preferences and deepest secrets before we ever meet face-to-face. Collecting personal information is significant at the beginning of a relationship, and obviously when you are first getting to know your partner, your interest level is high. Not only is this new person very compelling to you, but you are also trying to make a critical choice, so the more you know, the better. However, once that choice is made and you settle into the relationship, the "getting to know you" phase is set aside.

Although we will still learn a lot about our partner as we live life together, we often don't pursue that knowledge with the same intentionality that was used at the start. This can contribute to being lulled into the belief that you know all there is to know about your partner. This just isn't true! One of the best ways to stay engaged in your relationship is to remain vitally interested in your partner throughout your time together. Being curious about your partner's current thoughts, feelings, opinions, and how his or her perspectives are shifting is vital to a healthy couple relationship and maintaining a foundation of friendship. Don't get too comfortable in what you think you know!

Action

Do you know one of the best ways to make people like you? Let them talk about themselves. Really! If you meet someone for the first time and all you do is talk about yourself, the chances are high that when you leave, they won't remember much about you. However, spend that same time together asking them about who they are and what they think, and it's a safe bet that they will be looking forward to seeing you again. Being interested in others has a huge payoff. This follows suit in our couple relationships no matter how long we have been together. Staying inquisitive about who your partner is and what he or she thinks increases your relationship satisfaction with each other.

Here is a good way for you to connect, stay interested, and potentially learn something new. Create an opportunity to boost the good feelings in your relationship by interviewing each other with the Proust Questionnaire for Couples provided below. You could do this over a lazy Saturday morning breakfast, or maybe you want to go out and have a "get to know you all over again" dinner. Following are a few simple instructions to help make your interview session a great success:

- Take turns asking the questions. Each partner should interview the other using the complete questionnaire. By giving each other your full attention through each of the questions, you increase your feelings of being heard by one another.

- As you listen to each other's replies, be curious about the answers. Maybe you want to ask follow-up questions; you never know when a certain question may open the door for an enlightening conversation. You just may be surprised at what you learn and the good feelings that come with it.

As you answer the questions, don't overthink your replies. Often it is easiest to answer with the first idea or word that comes to mind.

{Reset Your Interest}

MUSCLE BUILDER
Proust Questionnaire for Couples

What is your idea of perfect happiness?

What is your greatest fear?

Which historical figure do you most identify with?

Which living person do you most admire?

What is the trait you most deplore in yourself?

What is the trait you most deplore in others?

What is your greatest extravagance?

What is your favorite journey?

What do you consider the most overrated virtue?

On what occasion do you lie?

What do you dislike the most about your appearance?

Which living person do you most despise?

Which words or phrases do you most overuse?

What is your greatest regret?

What or who is the greatest love of your life?

When and where were you the happiest?

Which talent would you most like to have?

What is your current state of mind?

If you could change one thing about yourself, what would it be?

If you could change one thing about your family, what would it be?

What do you consider your greatest achievement?

If you were to die and come back as a person or thing, what do you think it would be?

If you could choose what to come back as, what would it be?

What is your most treasured possession?

What do you regard as the lowest depth of misery?

Where would you like to live?

What is your favorite occupation?

What is your most marked characteristic?

What is the quality you most like in a man?

What is the quality you most like in a woman?

What do you most value in your friends?

Who are your favorite writers?

Who is your favorite hero of fiction?

Who are your heroes in real life?

What are your favorite names?

What is it that you most dislike?

How would you like to die?

What is your motto?

How Will "Keep It Interesting" Revolutionize Your Relationship?

Interviewing your partner allows both of you to focus on each other and learn something new. Letting the other person talk about themselves can increase a sense of connection. Really listening and being curious about their answers deepens your dialogue. Couples that stay vitally interested in each other maintain a foundation of friendship. This increases comfort, satisfaction, and pleasure in the relationship.

21

What about You?

Insight

We spend a lot of time and money in our culture promoting youth and avoiding aging. According to global anti-aging market research, the cost of our fascination with staying young and postponing death reached $281.6 billion in 2015 and is projected to hit $331.3 billion by 2020. It's as if collectively world citizens have agreed to avoid getting old at a great expense. I think this is because endings are scary. We simply cannot know or understand what it is like to die and what actually happens to us after death, which in turn invokes the typical reactions to any fear of the unknown: denial and avoidance. Yet ironically in a lifelong couple relationship, we commit to being there for one another during the fear of the unknown, which includes our final moments on earth. Death is a part of the agreement.

Not long ago, I had the privilege of meeting Lucille. She was eighty-five years old when we met and had lived in the same farm home for sixty-two years because she loved the privacy of the country. Her hair was striking silver and her eyes twinkled blue as the sea. When I met her, she had just celebrated her birthday, and this is what she told me: "Getting old is hard. You are young; enjoy life. Live every day like it is your last." This is a great reminder that getting close to the end often engages us more fully in the present. Sometimes when I say goodbye to my partner, I think if this were our last goodbye, have I loved him well and does he know it? If this was our final interaction on earth, is this what I want to leave him with?

What about You?

My grandparents had an epic romance. They met in 1941 as my grandpa was just heading off to serve in World War II as a naval pilot flying through the English Channel. He was dapper in his uniform, and my grandma was glamorous in her high heels. Apparently she had great "pins" or legs that caught my grandpa's eye. At the time they met, she was finishing Miss Wood's Kindergarten-Primary Training School, and later in her long career she would go on to become a nominated Minnesota Teacher of the Year. She was a gifted kindergarten teacher with patience to sit with any child learning to read, including me. A champion of learning, her large kindergarten room was full of spaces my grandpa built for the kids, from the trunk of Pooh's corner to a tree house full of pillows and books.

Together they raised four boys through the tumultuous years of the sixties and seventies, sending their oldest son off to Vietnam and, fortunately, welcoming him back home after his service was completed. With a clothing store on Main Street and a home that backed up to the high school football field, they maintained an upstanding presence in their small town. After years of hard work and robbing Peter to pay Paul, they acquired a beautiful log cabin in northern Minnesota. The lore goes that my grandpa, as a young boy attending Boy Scout camp, watched builders create that very cabin with the trees from the property. They went back years later and rented a cabin on the lake until fate would have it that they were able to buy the log cabin.

Much of my childhood was spent with them in that place making precious memories I have tucked away. But it was their relationship I remember most. They loved each other well and laughed a lot. Oh, I know they had worries, tensions, and family discord. Finances were tight sometimes and days were long, but their hearts were big, which made the troubles small. They by no means had it all together, but there was never a time I didn't witness affection between them and genuine care for one another. As my grandma aged, we would sit in the cabin kitchen talking for hours about life and her biggest fear: how it was all going to end. She worried about who was going to die first, and most of all, how my grandpa would be if she died before him. If you are in a committed couple relationship for a lifetime, these are ultimately the most pressing questions you will face. Eventually, unless your dates collide, one of you will exit first, leaving the other behind to hold the memories.

On a hot August day in 2003, my grandma fell. She had left the cabin to pick some flowers in the garden. As she fell, she hit her head, and her remaining moments of consciousness were few. My grandpa called for emergency help, and as they waited for the paramedics to come, she was barely holding on. It was during that moment of time that their life together, complete with all of their memories, was held in suspended animation. As my grandpa sat with her, they talked until there was no more time to give. Then, the last thing my grandma said to my grandpa was "What about you?" As he recollects that moment, it is with gratitude and amazement; it is evident that nothing in life has left a bigger impact on his soul than her simple, loving question, "What about you?"

Action

The question "What about you?" holds the ultimate hope for every couple and, I believe, the secret to a lifelong love affair. Most of the problems couples encounter come from spending too much time asking "What about me?" Often we are consumed with our own positions and personal satisfaction in our relationship, when just maybe, if *both* partners spent more days asking each other "What about you?" they would find a reciprocity of love that can last a lifetime. You never know the day your commitment will expire. I've watched friends lose their partners suddenly, and others who have endured a long goodbye. The one thing they have in common was the moment when they stood there alone, no longer a living couple. They would all say that moment came too soon.

When we are in the thick of it, though, the long-term, committed couple relationship can feel like it is going to last forever. We can easily feel justified in our frustrations, vindicated by our anger, and validated by our grievances. Yet the question remains: Are the frustrations, anger, and grievances really worth it in the long run? At the end of the day, I think Lucille was on to something. Growing old together is hard. That's why it is important to start being present for one another as soon as possible, loving each other well and living each day together as if it may be the last.

Keeping my grandma's question in mind, work through the following reflection with your partner. Can the two of you choose today to start asking "What about you?" in your relationship?

{Reset Your Perspective}

MUSCLE BUILDER
"What about You?"

1. If this was the last day with your partner . . .

    What would you want him or her to know?

    What would you do for him or her?

    What would you want to leave him or her with?

2. Why don't you take those actions every day?

This next week, start each day by looking at your partner and asking the question "What about you?" What does your partner need from you today, and how can you show up? (If you are not sure, *ask*!)

How Will What about You Revolutionize Your Relationship?

When you keep the end in mind, there is a powerful shift in the ability to appreciate your partner and be present. Living fully in the moment allows you to keep in perspective what really matters. Seeing your partner as your life traveler, the one who will be by your side until the end, elevates the importance of his or her presence in your life. You need each other. This is one of the most significant people in your world.

22

The Research Project

Life is really just a big experiment as we try to understand what brings us joy, what allows us to be the best version of ourselves, and what creates the most satisfying relationships. Look at this point in your couple relationship as a research project as you take action to reset your experiences with each other. By the time you're done experimenting with the Core Elements, Mind Benders, and Muscle Builders, these new actions will create a revolution you both need to feel better than ever before!

Now What?

Trying these approaches will give you a chance to understand yourself, shift your perspective, and assume your individual responsibility in your relationship. Likewise, it will make a difference for your partner and, in turn, will reenergize the relationship as a whole. Intimate relationships are systems, meaning that when one part changes, the other part has no choice but to react. So often people get frustrated with the relationship, and instead of being the change they wish to see in the relationship, they blame the other person and think, "If he/she would only change, everything would be fine." There is nothing more maddening than waiting around for someone or something outside of your control to change so your life can be better. As a matter of fact, that is the definition of a "victim mindset." If you want to reset your relationship, it starts with you. Or even better, it starts with both of you each taking responsibility for changing yourselves, not the other person.

What If None of This Stuff Works?

It is possible that after attempting to positively reset your relationship, you and your partner may be stuck. Things just are *not* changing! That is such a difficult, sad, and frustrating place to be when you really want things to change. There may be several contributors present in your relationship, preventing you from creating sustainable change. Often problems in life are like a jigsaw puzzle. As we attempt to put it together, some pieces are tough to figure out; we may think a blue piece is the sky when it is really the sea, or we may be missing pieces altogether. When this happens, it often takes a fresh set of eyes to look at the puzzle and point out what is missing. Sometimes couples have lived with their problems for so long or with such intensity that no matter how hard they try to figure things out together, they just can't get there. This is often an indicator that you need more help.

Four Critical Issues

Furthermore, as much as I would love to say that every couple relationship could experience positive changes, there are some issues that are going to require more intensive help first. One of my wisest mentors and a well-seasoned couples therapist, Steve McManus, LMFT, shared with me years ago that when couples are truly stuck, at minimum one of four issues might be occurring in their relationship. Throughout my work with couples, I have witnessed how not addressing these four critical issues inhibits partners from working with each other toward positive change. These are the four critical issues:

1. *Active addiction states of one or both partners.* This can include addiction to alcohol, drugs, sex, gambling, exercise, eating, and other such addictions that consume an individual and make them unavailable to their partner. Addiction is painful and takes an enormous toll on a couple's connection while creating negative generational implications for the whole family. There are so many good places to get help. Please don't wait any longer.

2. *Active and/or untreated mental health disorders.* This can include mood disorders (e.g., depression, anxiety, phobias, bipolar disorder, etc.); pervasive personality disorders (e.g., borderline, dependent, paranoid, narcissistic, etc.) and/or other mental health concerns (like ADD/ADHD). When undiagnosed and/or untreated, not only do individuals suffer unnecessarily, but so does the relationship. Due to the stigma that still exists around mental health, many people delay treating manageable disorders. Go see a mental health professional and stop your struggle.

3. *Active infidelity.* This includes emotional and physical affairs, both in reality and in virtual environments (i.e., online, texting, etc.). If you or your partner's head and heart are somewhere else, your relationship isn't going to be the first priority. There is a variety of reasons partners may choose to have an affair, but they all have one thing in common—they are an indicator that the committed primary relationship needs help. The result of an affair is deception and betrayal. Both of these experiences are painful realities to live in that take a toll on your body, mind,

and spirit. Deciding to end the affair game is good for everyone involved.

4. *Active and/or untreated domestic violence.* This includes physical abuse, sexual abuse, emotional abuse, and psychological abuse that is ongoing and/or has never been addressed. Being hit, threatened, forced, manipulated, used, yelled at, and depreciated are forms of abusive and unacceptable behavior. Domestic violence affects men and women of all cultures and socioeconomic status. It is not healthy, and it is *never* a form of love. If you are experiencing abuse in any form and need help, contact TheHotline.org.

Look at the Issues This Way

In 2009 I started to get sick; it was nothing notable, but it seemed like I picked up every cold, and it usually manifested into a sinus infection. By 2010 it seemed like I had one continuous cold/sinus infection coupled with constant coughing and lingering fatigue. During this time, I made multiple trips to my general physician; two ear, nose, and throat specialists; and one allergist, trying to figure out what was wrong. I received no concrete answers and too many unnecessary prescriptions to count. By the winter of 2011 this mysterious illness caused such violent coughing I broke a rib and, subsequently, experienced strange pains in my abdomen for months. This increased doctor visits, scans, and proposed origins, but there was still no diagnosis.

The spring came, and my anxiety increased. I worried that after this long, doctors would either think I was crazy or there was something really wrong that just hadn't been uncovered. By August of 2011, my eyesight started to change, along with the appearance of my right eye. I went to the eye doctor, and he gave me glasses. They never worked. Shortly after that, I was once again online searching my list of symptoms and came across the blog of a woman describing my story almost verbatim. After reading what she wrote, I knew what I was dealing with. That week I secured an appointment with another ear, nose, and throat specialist, went in, and immediately asked for an MRI. I told him my long story and that I believed I had silent sinus syndrome. He appeased my request for an MRI. I left the office and two hours later got a call. He said, "You have the biggest mass on the right side of your face that I have seen in ten years. You need to come back in immediately." The next day I saw the doctor. He told me that he would like to do surgery right away because this was an urgent concern that was not going to get better on its own. After two years of struggling, I finally found the answer I had been looking for. I had the surgery and am happy to report that I am in great health.

Why am I telling you this story? Because relational health problems and physical health problems aren't all that different. Relationship problems can often drag out for a long time and cause us to seek many solutions as we try to figure out what is really wrong. If any of the four critical issues—addiction, mental health concerns, infidelity, or abuse—resonate with you, your partner, and your relationship, think of me as the doctor saying, "You need surgery now, because these urgent concerns are not going to get better on their own." Actually, waiting any longer will allow them to get even worse and create bigger problems in the long run. If you haven't been feeling right about what's going on in your relationship or have been looking for help in multiple ways and trying to self-diagnose and treat these issues on your own without any success, go to the right professional today. If you have vacillated between feeling like you are crazy or wondering if something is really wrong, you're not crazy—go with your gut, advocate for your relationship, and get an expert opinion.

If you are experiencing any of the four critical issues in your relationship, it is recommended that you attend first to treating and resolving the primary concern(s) before entering into work on your couple relationship. This doesn't mean you ignore your couple relationship, it just means that until you and/or your partner is fully available for the relationship, positive, sustainable change is going to be difficult to obtain. Making a consultation call to get some direction on how to pursue help for these concerns is an excellent reason to contact a couples therapist. Do not hesitate.

Getting Help

Finding a professional couples therapist is nothing to be embarrassed about. Think of it this way—you would never buy a car and expect it to drive for years without taking good care of it. For your car to continue operating well, you must put gas in it, wash it, change the oil, and replace the brakes and tires. If your car broke down and you didn't know how to fix it, you wouldn't leave it on the side of the road. You would find someone who could tell you what was going on and what could be done to get it operating again. Yet we often put more discipline and money into maintaining our cars than we do our most significant relationships. If you can't find your way to a satisfying relationship on your own, take it to a specialist. That's what you would do for your car. Need I say more?

How Do We Find a Great Couples Therapist?

"How do we find a great couples therapist?" is not a dumb question. I repeat, this is not a stupid thing to wonder. It isn't easy to find a couples therapist if you don't know what to look for and what to ask. Also, not all therapists are trained to work with couples even if they say they "do" couples therapy. Couples therapy is one of the hardest modes of therapy to deliver well, and therapists need specific training to ensure they are providing the best possible service to their clients. After over a decade studying, practicing, and educating graduate school students in the art and science of performing couples therapy, I have come to understand that three key pieces are critical to receiving good couples therapy:

1. *Systemic thinking.* It is imperative that a couple's therapist thinks systemically, meaning they see the couple as having multiple individual parts while also being part of a collective whole. They need to be able to strategize and synthesize with all of these parts and work with care for each individual while keeping the relationship top of mind. This requires excellent skills in joining with each partner and balancing attention to all aspects of the relationship without bias.

   Ask potential therapists: Can you describe for me systemic thinking, and is that how you approach working with couples? Can you give me an example of how you take care of each partner while also paying attention to the relationship?

2. *Specific training.* Many therapy programs include one class in couples therapy, and this is not enough. For real competency, therapists need to have further and specific training in the variety of couples issues and the best practice ways to approach those concerns. If a couples therapist has had further training, it can be helpful for you to review the concepts and philosophies of how they have been trained.

   Ask potential therapists: Can you please tell me your specific training beyond graduate school that helps you work with couples? What is your philosophy of working with relationships? Is there a particular model or theory you use?

3. *Specialty focus.* For a therapist to be excellent at working with couples and their concerns, the couple relationship needs to be their specialty, meaning they have logged many hours working with couples. They need to have a practice set up to meet the needs of couples and also have an understanding of the ethical dilemmas that couples present. Also, they need to be in the "flow" of the work, doing it day in and day out, sharp and on their game.

Ask potential therapists: Is working with couples your specialty? How long and how often do you work with couples? Do you have the time to take on a new couple? Have you worked with (your specific concern) before?

Other Important Questions

1. *Do you use any assessments to help you understand couple relationships better?* Appropriate assessments can be very useful in providing greater detail and a deeper look into your circumstances.

2. *Do you collaborate with other therapists, caregivers, and/or treatment centers to help us get the best care possible?* If your circumstances require it, collaborative care can speed up services and gets all of your care providers on the same page.

3. *Are you accessible for us to reach if we need in-the-moment help with a conflict or crisis?* Some couples may benefit from real-time coaching through issues, and having access to the couples therapist outside of sessions can be very helpful.

4. *Do you provide virtual sessions or support through virtual modalities like apps, texting, videoconferences, etc.?* If you have obstacles to meeting face-to-face, look for a couples therapist that

can provide virtual solutions for sessions.

5. Do you offer packages for services or provide intensive sessions if needed? Both time and money matter when it comes to focusing on making progress, and many couples therapists offer options that address both of these concerns.

6. And most importantly, do you like being a couples therapist? Being a couples therapist is difficult and is best done by a professional who genuinely believes they are called to the work.

The Hardest Step Is the First One

For many couples, the most difficult part of getting help is making the initial contact and setting up an appointment. Getting through this milestone can be anxiety provoking and create a sense of shame or failure for couples. Please don't let those feelings get the better of you. Attending to your relationship is hands-down one of the biggest gifts you can give each other. Until you do that, you will be walking in the shadow lands together with the real potential of your union unknown. By opening yourself up to seeing a couples specialist, you will bring into the light the very fears that are holding you at odds today. Similar to ripping off a bandage, it may hurt initially, but by addressing it head on, you can quickly find relief. Be brave for your relationship.

Resources for Finding a Couples Therapist

www.therapistlocator.net
www.goodtherapy.org
www.psychologytoday.com

Conclusion

A Swan Story

A handful of animals mate for life, and swans are one of them. Swans are known to stay together for a lifetime in an animal kingdom version of a "committed" relationship, which can last up to thirty years. They are also known to grieve when they lose their mates, and never pick another partner. Every pair of swans has a story of how they met and mated, where they lived and raised their young, and how they eventually grew old together while weathering the storms of life. They are a natural inspiration in a time when the prevalence of divorce in America is still impacting a large portion of the population.

There are a myriad of reasons why divorce has become more common, from societal normalization and diminished stigmas that used to be widespread, to broad changes in the moral structure of our culture and reduced adherence to religious constructs, to increased financial, educational, and vocational equality between men and women. And sometimes divorce is a necessary path out of a painful or destructive relationship. But moreover, I think a stronger contribution can be attributed to the expectation that one person is supposed to be our perfect everything: perfect lover; perfect companion; perfect partner; perfect provider; and even a perfect parent. We want our partner to be it all rather than being human, and these are impossible expectations.

In much the same way that the media has generated a luxury mindset of the middle class, making it seem attainable for all people to have huge, new, beautifully furnished homes, expensive cars, big jewelry, on-trend wardrobes, and island vacations, it has also portrayed an idealized love relationship that should meet all of our expectations. When those expectations are not fulfilled, we react by searching for the next relationship that is bound to perfectly meet our vision of what "should be." In turn, we want things that aren't realistic, and when they don't come easily, we think we need to look elsewhere. We are hunting for a unicorn, and unlike swans, unicorns don't exist.

Our Swan Story—Chasing Sunshine

In the spring of 1990, my partner Jess and I drove south. This is a typical reaction for most people after living through a Minnesota winter. After long months of freezing temperatures, piles of snow, and the sun setting at four p.m., even Kansas City in March can feel like a tropical paradise to a Minnesotan. Backtracking a bit, Jess and I had met in the fall on a blind date. We were both attending a small private college in Minneapolis where it was common to have mixers on the weekend and for roommates to organize meet-ups for people to connect. One particular weekend, he was on a compassion date with a friend's little sister, and I was helping organize the event. We ended up at the same party afterward, and although we never talked, we definitely noticed each other. A few weeks later there was another mixer, and this time my roommate set us up. We spent the night talking like old friends that hadn't seen each other in ages. I remember there was a familiarity in his hands and a kindness in his eyes I seemed to recollect, even though we had never met before. I would find out later that he went home that night and wrote in his journal that he had just met the woman he was going to marry. This was our "meet-cute," and it was movie worthy in our minds. We starting dating immediately and made it through the winter, which I know went faster than most thanks to falling in love. By spring, we wanted to get away, so we decided to drive south until we could roll the windows down. We were chasing sunshine. Little did we know this would be the motto for our life together.

We married in the summer of 1991, a big *Father of the Bride* wedding full of friends, family, music, and optimistic ideals of what marriage would be like. The night before our wedding, my Mom said to me, "You don't have to get married if you don't want to. You are really young." I suppose this could have offended me, but I understood. My parents married young, and she had some wisdom about that choice. However, my response was this: "I know, Mom. But I found my person. I would rather grow up with him than grow up and try to find him again." Little did I know what I was saying, and grow up we did. By the end of the first year, we both wondered where our optimistic ideals had gone. Being married was harder than we thought, as it is for most people. The first year is one of the toughest, and in that year we had our initial experience with a couples therapist. We learned a lot about each other and realized that while it may be possible to project perfection to the outside world, that was not a sustainable way to try to live together in reality. We made some adjustments, and our relationship continued on.

Unfortunately, at that time we weren't ready to get to the heart of our issues. You see, although we both grew up in loving families that gave many assets to our relationship, we also acquired liabilities that were getting in our way. We had been taught different conflict styles, played with a variety of Drama patterns, and ironically, both became young caretakers in families experiencing grief and loss. On top of that, we were each nurtured in conservative religious communities that encouraged compliance to predetermined beliefs and denial of personal doubts. All of this contributed to some distorted ideas about our individual identities and how we were "supposed to be" in the world. Together these liabilities worked to build a cellophane wall between us where we could see and even touch each other but not really feel each other. Because of this unconscious arrangement, by the end of year three, we were burning out.

We knew early on that we may never have children, and at that point, it was proving to be true. I was working without a whole lot of purpose for a Fortune 500 company, and Jess was overcommitted as a teacher, coaching and leading outside of the classroom while simultaneously going to graduate school. We began to live parallel lives and started to lose each other. I clearly remember the day I went to him and said, "This isn't working. I would like it to, but I don't know what to do." He told me, "I know—I will do anything it takes." We went back to our couples therapist. This time, we got to the heart of it. The defining moment was when we both looked at each other and admitted we were stuck, disconnected, and hopeless. We still took the vows we made seriously but didn't have any idea where to go from there. It was an "I want to be with you but don't know how to be with you" moment, unaware that we were in the midst of a major change. Both of us were questioning our identities and the relationship, wondering if it was all still meant to be. We decided to take some time and see if we could change together; after all, our commitment to the relationship was still strong. This was our turning point. So, once again, we got into the car, put the windows down, and decided to chase sunshine.

The next year was spent driving weekly to couples therapy and working hard on our relationship. We explored everything from who we were to how we were raised, how we fought, how we made love, and, most importantly, what we wanted in life and how we wanted to get there. Through this process, our life together transformed. All our thoughts, feelings, issues, and concerns about the relationship went on the table because there was nothing left to lose.

New habits, riskier communication, and true vulnerability were hard fought and eventually achieved. And through it all, love was found anew, deeper, and more real than anything we had each known before. A new relationship started. In four short years, we had been through all six stages of the change cycle, and we were on our way to another round.

That was twenty-one years ago, and there have been many more rounds over the years, some quick and fun, some long and arduous, but none as significant as the first. Working hard to make it through the first years rebuilt our foundation and gave us something solid to build on going forward. Since that time, we have enjoyed the miracle of having two beautiful children. Both conceptions were stories of surprise and unexpected change, just like the incredible and challenging journey of raising them. We have had seasons of great gain and times of distinct loss. We have experienced the joy of family and friends, mourned the death of family and friends, and navigated the tensions of family and friends. We have achieved significant accomplishments, given up unproductive dreams, and rearranged careers. We have moved, built, sold, simplified, and filled albums of memories with ordinary moments and epic adventures. We have not done it perfect, right, or clean. Love is messy, and we have just done it together one season at a time. Through it all, we have trusted the process and believed *in* each other and *for* each other as stewards of each other's souls. And we aren't done yet—we are still chasing sunshine.

At the beginning of the book, I told you that if I couldn't show you how I have authentically lived what I am writing, there would be a missing piece in this book. Even though I have worked with many couples over the years and have seen dramatic, life-changing, and love-giving transformations, nothing is as convincing to me as my own experience. I know what it feels like to be hopeless and want things to change. I know what it feels like to think things can't change. And I know what it feels like for things to change and become better than you ever thought possible. I know that a revolution in a relationship can be a reality if *both of you want it, are willing to get support,* and *are ready to work together.* What I have written for you is what I wish someone had given to me and Jess years ago. It is life-tested. It does work.

What's Your Swan Story?

Now it's up to you. Truly, you can lead a horse to water, but you cannot make it drink. My hope is that you drink the water in this book—every last drop of it. Use the Core Elements to get real about your relationship. Just because it is hard at times doesn't mean it isn't meant to be. Grab onto the insights, and become a relationship expert about your partner and your commitment. Really work at the Mind Benders. Become the primary operator of your thoughts and emotions. Increase your ability to self-regulate, communicate, and effectively shift your experiences. Lean into the Muscle Builders, and gain strength in your relationship. Create the kind of partnership that can be sustained over time and is resilient. Together you have the power to make your life with one another not just good, but great. Get more support if you need it, and don't be shy about it—your relationship matters.

A Final Note

Dear Reader,

You did it! You made it all the way through the life changing information that can create a Revolution in Your Relationship. What an amazing accomplishment. Before you close this book, take the time to do one more exercise.

On the next page is a Relationship Reset Pledge. Once you both feel you have taken in everything your relationship needs from this book, create a moment and speak the pledge to one another. Take turns reading it out loud, just like commitment vows. You can simply do it in the middle of your kitchen or formally proclaim it in a ceremony with your family and friends. But do it. Then, post the pledge somewhere you can see it every day as a reminder of your revolution.

Believing in Your Love for a Lifetime,

Jen Elmquist

P.S. Want to continue to grow with Relationship Reset? Join us online at jenelmquist.com

Relationship Reset Pledge

In Our Relationship, I Choose to:

Pursue Alignment by striving to get on the same page, finding our way to a common goal, and creating together a vision for the future, knowing that a house divided cannot stand the tests of time.

Build Reciprocity by giving fully to our relationship my very best and wanting, with my whole heart, for each of us to become the best versions of ourselves in our life together.

Instill Trust by remembering that we are on the same team and we have each other's back.
I will create a safe place to be honest and vulnerable.
I will not take advantage of you.
The only way we win is together.

Activate Love on a daily basis, not just the feeling word of falling in love, but also the action word of commitment to love.
I will seek to act kindly, softly, and justly with you and for you.

By these actions, I pledge to Revolutionize our Relationship For You, For Me, and For Us.

Research and Resources

AASECT: American Association of Sexuality Educators, Counselors and Therapists. Retrieved 18 April 2016, from http://www.aasect.org.

Adler, A., & Brett, C. (1997). *Understanding life: An introduction to the psychology of Alfred Adler.* Oxford, England: Oneworld.

Ainsworth, M., Blehar, M., Waters, E., & Wall, S. (1978). *Patterns of attachment: A psychological study of the strange situation.* Hillsdale, NJ: Lawrence Erlbaum Associates.

Bach, D. (2001). *Smart couples finish rich: 9 Steps to creating a rich future for you and your partner.* New York, NY: Broadway Books.

Beck, A. (1988). *Love is never enough: How couples can overcome misunderstandings, resolve conflicts, and solve relationship problems through cognitive therapy.* New York, NY: Harper & Row.

Berne, E. (1964). *Games people play: The psychology of human relationships.* New York, NY: Grove Press, Inc.

Black, D. R., Gleser, L. J., & Kooyers, K. J. (1990). A meta-analytic evaluation of couples weight-loss programs. *Health Psychology,* 9(3), 330-347.

Boswell, N. (1977). *TA for busy people: How to use transactional analysis at home and at work.* New York, NY: Harper & Row.

Boszormenyi-Nagy, I. & Spark, G. (1973). *Invisible loyalties: Reciprocity in intergenerational family therapy.* Hagerstown, MD: Harper & Row.

Bowen, M. (1978). *Family therapy in clinical practice.* New York, NY: J. Aronson.

Bowlby, J. (1969). *Attachment and loss.* New York, NY: Basic Books.

Bridges, W. (1980). *Transitions: Making sense of life's changes.* Reading, MA: Addison-Wesley.

Busby, D., & Holman, T. (2009). Perceived match or mismatch on the Gottman conflict styles: Associations with relationship outcome variables. *Family Process,* 48(4), 531-545. http://dx.doi.org/10.1111/j.1545-5300.2009.01300.x.

Campbell, J. (1972). *The hero with a thousand faces.* Princeton, NJ: Princeton University Press.

Chamney, M. (2010). Book review: The science of compassionate love: Theory, research, and applications edited by Fehr, B., Sprecher, S., & Underwood, L. *Journal of Renal Care,* 36(1), 54. http://dx.doi.org/10.1111/j.1755-6686.2010.00144_2.x.

Coontz, S. (2005). *Marriage, a history: From obedience to intimacy or how love conquered marriage.* New York, NY: Viking Penguin.

The Couples Institute: Online couples' community. (2013). Retrieved from http://www.thecouplesinstitute.com.

DeSilver, D., & DeSilver, D. (2014). *5 Facts about love and marriage.*

Pew Research Center. Retrieved 7 November 2015, from http://www.pewresearch.org/fact-tank/2014/02/14/5-facts-about-love-and-marriage/.

Dikker, S., Silbert, L., Hasson, U., & Zevin, J. (2014). On the same wavelength: Predictable language enhances speaker-listener brain-to-brain synchrony in posterior superior temporal gyrus. *The Journal of Neuroscience*, 34(18), 6267-6272. http://dx.doi.org/10.1523/jneurosci.3796-13.2014.

Doss, B. D., Atkins, D. C., & Christensen, A. (2003). Who's dragging their feet? Husbands and wives seeking marital therapy. *Journal of Marital and Family Therapy*, 29(2), 165-177. doi:10.1111/j.1752-0606.2003.tb01198.x.

Dyer, W. (2007). *Change your thoughts, change your life: Living the wisdom of the Tao*. Carlsbad, CA: Hay House, Inc.

Ellis, A. (2004). *Rational emotive behavior therapy: It works for me—it can work for you*. Amherst, NY: Prometheus Books.

Erikson, E. H., & Erikson, J. M. (1997). *The life cycle completed*. New York, NY: W.W. Norton & Company, Inc.

Feige, K. (Producer), & Black, S. (Director). (2013). *Ironman 3* (Motion picture). United States: Walt Disney Studios Motion Pictures.

Fincham, F., & Beach, S. (2014). I say a little prayer for you: Praying for partner increases commitment in romantic relationships. *Journal of Family Psychology*, 28(5), 587-593. http://dx.doi.org/10.1037/a0034999.

FinishRich Media. (1997). Retrieved 8 November 2015, from http://www.finishrich.com/free_resources/fr_home.php.

Fisher, H. (2004). *Why we love: The nature and chemistry of romantic love.* New York, NY: Henry Holt and Company, LLC.

Fisher, H. (2015). The brain in love. Ted.com. Retrieved 7 November 2015, from https://www.ted.com/talks/helen_fisher_studies_the_brain_in_love?language=en.

Frankl, V. (2006). *Man's search for meaning.* Boston, MA: Beacon Press.

Friel, J., & Friel, L. (1988). *Adult children: The secrets of dysfunctional families.* Pompano Beach, FL: Health Communications, Inc.

Goleman, D. (1995). *Emotional intelligence.* New York, NY: Bantam Dell.

Gottman Institute. (2015). Retrieved 7 November 2015, from https://www.gottman.com.

Gottman, J. M. (2011). *The science of trust: Emotional attunement for couples.* New York: W.W. Norton.

Gottman, J. M., & Silver, N. (1994). *Why marriages succeed or fail: What you can learn from the breakthrough research to make your marriage last.* New York: Simon & Schuster.

Hanson, R. (2015). Retrieved 8 November 2015, from https://www.rickhanson.net

Hanson, R., & Mendius, R. (2009). *Buddha's brain: The practical neuroscience of happiness, love, & wisdom.* Oakland, CA: New Harbinger Publications.

Hardy, N., Soloski, K., Ratcliffe, G., Anderson, J., & Willoughby, B. (2014). Associations between family of origin climate, relationship self-regulation, and marital outcomes. *Journal of Marital & Family Therapy*, 41(4), 508-521. http://dx.doi.org/10.1111/jmft.12090.

Hendrix, H. (1988). *Getting the love you want: A guide for couples.* New York, NY, NY: Henry Holt and Company, LLC.

Holman, T., & Jarvis, M. (2003). Hostile, volatile, avoiding, and validating couple-conflict types: An investigation of Gottman's couple-conflict types. *Personal Relationships*, 10(2), 267-282. http://dx.doi.org/10.1111/1475-6811.00049.

Horney, K. (1950). *Neurosis and human growth: The struggle toward self-realization.* New York, NY, NY: W. W. Norton & Company, Inc.

Hudson, F. (1999). *The adult years: Mastering the art of self-renewal.* San Francisco, CA: Jossey-Bass.

Institute of Noetic Sciences. (2016). Ongoing research-the love study. Retrieved 13 April 2016, from http://www.livingdeeply.org.

Jack, S. (2005). *Study of couple relationships.* Lecture, Saint Mary's University, Minneapolis, MN.

Jacobson, N., & Gurman, A. (1995). *Clinical handbook of couple therapy.* New York, NY: The Guilford Press.

Johnson, S. (2008). *Hold me tight: Seven conversations for a lifetime of love.* New York, NY: Little, Brown and Company.

Karpman, S. (2010). Karpman Drama Triangle. Retrieved 3 March 2015, from http://karpmandramatriangle.com.

Karremans, J., Van Lange, P., Ouwerkerk, J., & Kluwer, E. (2003).

When forgiving enhances psychological well-being: The role of interpersonal commitment. *Journal of Personality and Social Psychology*, 84(5), 1011.-1026. http://dx.doi.org/10.1037/0022-3514.84.5.1011

Kusner, K., Mahoney, A., Pargament, K., & DeMaris, A. (2014). Sanctification of marriage and spiritual intimacy predicting observed marital interactions across the transition to parenthood. *Journal of Family Psychology*, 28(5), 604-614. http://dx.doi.org/10.1037/a0036989.

Light, A., & Fitzsimons, G. (2014). Contextualizing marriage as a means and a goal. *Psychological Inquiry*, 25(1), 88-94. http://dx.doi.org/10.1080/1047840x.2014.878522.

Mahoney, A., & Cano, A. (2014). Introduction to the special section on religion and spirituality in family life: Delving into relational spirituality for couples. *Journal of Family Psychology*, 28(5), 583-586. http://dx.doi.org/10.1037/fam0000030

Mahoney, A., & Cano, A. (2014). Introduction to the special section on religion and spirituality in family life: Pathways between relational spirituality, family relationships and personal well-being. *Journal of Family Psychology*, 28(6), 735-738. http://dx.doi.org/10.1037/fam0000041.

McCraty, R., Atkinson, M., Tomasino, D., & Bradley, R. (2006). *The coherent heart: Heart-brain interactions, psychophysiological coherence and the emergence of system-wide order*. Boulder Creek, CA: Institute of HeartMath.

Myss, C. (2002). *Sacred contracts: Awakening your divine potential*. New York, NY: Harmony Books.

National Domestic Violence Hotline. (2015). Retrieved 7 November 2015, from http://www.thehotline.org.

Neto, F. (2012). Compassionate love for a romantic partner, love styles, and subjective well-being. *Interpersona: An International Journal on Personal Relationships*, 6(1), 23-39. http://dx.doi.org/10.5964/ijpr.v6i1.88

Normans Media Ltd. (2016, March 18). Anti-aging products and services report 2016: The global market to 2020 for the $300+ billion industry. *M2 Press WIRE*.

Notarius, C., & Markman, H (1993). *We can work it out: Making sense of marital conflict*. New York: Putnam.

O'Hanlon, B. (2000). *Do one thing different: Ten simple ways to change your life*. New York, NY: Quill.

Omaha, J. (2004). *Psychotherapeutic interventions for emotion regulation: EMDR and bilateral stimulation for affect management*. New York, NY: W.W. Norton & Company, Inc.

Open Culture. (2015). *Marcel Proust fills out a questionnaire in 1890: The manuscript of the "Proust Questionnaire."* Retrieved 8 November 2015, from http://www.openculture.com/2014/06/the-manuscript-of-the-proust-questionnaire.html.

Owen, J., Rhoades, G., & Stanley, S. (2013). Sliding versus deciding in relationships: Associations with relationship quality, commitment, and infidelity. *Journal of Couple & Relationship Therapy*, 12(2), 135-149. http://dx.doi.org/10.1080/15332691.2013.779097.

Porges, S. (2011). *The polyvagal theory: Neurophysiological foundations of emotions, attachment, communication, and self-regulation*. New

York, NY: W. W. Norton & Company, Inc.

Quinby, L. (2013). TA tutor: Transactional analysis tools for psychotherapy. Retrieved from http://ta-tutor.com.

Raffel, L. (1999). *Should I stay or go?: How controlled separation (CS) can save your marriage.* Lincolnwood, IL: Contemporary Books.

Reticular Activating System. (2015). Retrieved 8 November 2015, from http://www.reticularactivatingsystem.org.

Sabey, A., Rauer, A., & Jensen, J. (2014). Compassionate love as a mechanism linking sacred qualities of marriage to older couples' marital satisfaction. *Journal of Family Psychology*, 28(5), 594-603. http://dx.doi.org/10.1037/a0036991.

Satir, V. (1991). *The Satir model: Family therapy and beyond.* Palo Alto, CA: Science and Behavior Books.

Schnarch, D. M. (2009). *Passionate marriage: Love, sex, and intimacy in emotionally committed relationships.* New York, NY: W.W. Norton.

Seligman, M. (2000). Optimism, pessimism, and mortality. *Mayo Clinic Proceedings*, 75(2), 133-134. http://dx.doi.org/10.4065/75.2.133.

Seligman, M. (2002). *Authentic happiness: Using the new positive psychology to realize your potential for lasting fulfillment.* New York, NY: Free Press.

Seligman, M. (2004). Can happiness be taught? *Daedalus*, 133(2), 80-87. http://dx.doi.org/10.1162/001152604323049424.

Seligman, M. (2008). Positive health. *Applied Psychology*, 57(s1),

3-18. http://dx.doi.org/10.1111/j.1464-0597.2008.00351.x.

Sheehy, G. (1976). *Passages*. New York, NY: E. P. Dutton.

Siegel, D. (2010). *Mindsight: The new science of personal transformation*. New York, NY: Bantam Books.

Substance Abuse and Mental Health Services Administration.(2015). SAMHSA's national helpline. Retrieved 7 November 2015, from http://www.samhsa.gov/find-help/national-helpline.

Silver, J. (Producer), & The Wachowski Brothers (Director). (1999). *The Matrix* (Motion picture). United States: Warner Bros.

Walsh, D. (2004). *Why do they act that way?: A survival guide to the adolescent brain for you and your teen*. New York, NY: Free Press.

Willard, D. (1999). *Hearing God: Developing a conversational relationship with God*. Downers Grove, IL: InterVarsity Press.

INDEX

A

accounting, 147-153

addictions, 215

The Adolescent. See The Bully

affairs, 33, 43-44, 215-217

alignment, 43, 177, 183-184, 188, 191, 230

Amen, Daniel, 120

anger. See conflict styles

annoying behaviors, 138-139

anxiety, 33, 36, 53, 94, 215, 221

assessment, 45-47, 110-115

attaching, 12, 14-18, 40-41, 54

attention, focusing on partner, 133-136

The Authentic Ally, 62, 85

B

The Baby

generally, 58

as Authentic Ally, 85

The Baby/Baby Pattern, 76-77

The Buddy/Baby Pattern, 64-67

The Bully/Baby Pattern, 69-71

Bach, David, 183

The Bad Parent. See The Bully

Bader, Ellyn, 107

balanced state, 49-51

base thoughts, 142-146

Berne, Eric, 55

blended families, 17-20, 39

bonding, 176

Boszormenyi-Nagy, Ivan, 147

boundaries, 21, 62, 73, 82, 161

Bowen, Murray, 28

the brain, 119-121, 142, 170

brain workout, 121-125

Bridges, William, 32

The Buddy

generally, 57

The Buddy/Baby Pattern, 64-67

The Buddy/Buddy Pattern, 71-74

The Buddy/Bully Pattern, 67-69

as Curious Collaborator, 84

The Bully

generally, 58-59

The Buddy/Bully Pattern, 67-69

The Bully/Baby Pattern, 69-71

The Bully/Bully Pattern, 74-76

as Persistent Partner, 85

C

careers, 16, 21-26, 29-30

changes, 9-11, 31-36, 39. See also Six-Stage Change Cycle

Chardin, Pierre Teilhard de, 189

The Child. See The Baby

children, 9, 19-20, 24-27, 30, 42-44. See also blended families

Clean Slate Protocol, 159-162

Committed Couple Relationships Chart, 46

communication. See also conflict styles

during the attachment stage, 15-18

during the integrating stage, 35-36

interpersonal communication, 169-173

Pre-Talk Thought, 141-146

and self-disclosure, 110-115

compassion, 195-200

conflict styles

generally, 89-93

benefit of similarity, 96-97

Common Conflict Styles for Committed Couples, 99-100

The Demander, 93-94

The Destroyer, 95-96

The Disappearer, 95

The Discusser, 93

The Distancer, 94

The Humble Warrior, 101-107

Is This Normal Exercise, 99-100

learned affect, 90-91

learning to fight better, 100-107

The Matrix Effect, 100-101

overreacting styles, 94-96

and patterns, 53

pursue/distance adaptation, 97-99

typical styles, 93-94

understanding differences, 97

Core Elements, generally, 2-3, 7

counseling, 214-221

The Crazy Caretakers, 72-74

critical issues, 214-218

critical thinking, 141-146

The Culture Clash, 74-76

curiosity, 128-132, 139, 201-206

The Curious Collaborator, 61, 84

cycles. See also Six-Stage Change Cycle

generally, 9-11

D

D-Factor (differentiating), 28-34, 43-44, 53-54

Deal Breakers, 138-139

death, 207-211

The Demander, 93-94

depression, 33, 36, 186, 215

The Destroyer, 95-96

differentiating, 28-34, 43-44, 53-54

The Disappearer, 95-96

The Discusser, 93

The Distancer, 94

divorce, 33, 36, 223

domestic violence, 216
The Drama Dance Pattern, 77-80
Drama Patterns, 64-81, 83-85
Drama Roles, 56-60
Drama Triangle, 55-56
Durable Patterns, 81-85
Durable Roles, 61-63
Durable Triangle, 55-56

E

Ellis, Albert, 137
emotional experiences, 90, 110-115
empathy, 59, 92, 142-143
the end, keeping in mind, 207-211
The Epic Kiss, 165-167
establishing, 18-22, 41
expectations, releasing, 137-140

F

families, merging, 17-20, 39
Family Ledger, 147-153
family of origin, 18, 30, 54, 60, 77, 90, 96, 147-150, 175
focus, 155-158
forgiveness, 45, 104, 148-153
Frankl, Viktor, 109-110
friends, 30, 160-161, 206

G

gender roles, 52
Gottman, John, 91, 165
gratitude, 150-153, 158
Growing Pains, 81-83

H

Hanson, Rick, 120
help, 214-221
homeostasis, 49-51
The Humble Warrior, 101-107, 149
humility, 102

I

I and I (individuating), 22-24, 41-42
identity development (individual), 11, 26. See also D-Factor (differentiating)
individuating (I and I), 22-24, 41-42
infidelity, 33, 43-44, 215-217
The Inside Scale, 110-113
integrating, 34-38, 44-45
intimacy, 72-74, 165-167, 177-181
Is This Normal? Exercises
Predictable Patterns in Committed Couple Relationships, 87
Six-Stage Change Cycle of Committed Couple Relationships, 47

J

Jack, Susan, 39

judgments and judging, 127-132

K

Karpman, Stephen, 55

kindness, 195-200

kissing, 165-167

L

Law of Attraction, 155-158

Lazar, Sara, 190

ledgers, 147-153

limits, 138-140

A Loving Observer, 127-132, 139, 161

M

The Matrix Effect, 100-101

McManus, Steve, 214

meditation, 190-191

mental health disorders, 215

midlife meltdown, 65-67

Mind Benders, generally, 3, 117

miscommunication, 170-173

Missed Moments, 69-71

mood disorders, 215

Muscle Builders, generally, 4, 163

N

negative thoughts, 119-125

neuroscience, 119-121

neutral zone in transition, 32

O

Omaha, John, 90-91

The Outside Scale, 110-111, 113-115

over focusing on relationship, 16

The Overfunctioning Partner. See The Buddy; The Bully

overpersonalizing, 139

P

The Parent. See The Buddy

parenting, 19-20, 24. See also children

patterns

generally, 49-51

Drama patterns, 64-81

from Drama to Durable, 83-85

Durable patterns, 81-83

emotional reasons for, 53-55

functional reasons for, 51-52

identifying your patterns, 86

Is This Normal? Exercise, 87

predictable patterns, 87

and roles, 57-64

understanding, 55-56

Pearson, Pete, 107

The Persecutor. See The Bully

The Persistent Partner, 62-63, 85

personal assessment, 110-115

Personal Limits, 138-140

personality disorders, 215

prayer, 190-193

Predictable Patterns in Committed Couple Relationships, 87

Predictive Listening, 170

Pre-Talk Thought, 141-146

prioritizing your relationship, 159-162

Proust Questionnaire for Couples, 201-205

purpose, 186-188

pursue/distance adaptation, 97-99

Q

Quinby, Lewis, 55

R

Raffel, Lee, 36

reflections, 196-198

relationship contract, 21

Relationship Reset Pledge, 229-230

Relationship Vision Statement, 187-188

relationships

changes in, 9-11, 31-36, 39

cycles, 9-11. See also Six-Stage Change Cycle

over focusing on, 16

as research projects, 213-221

Releasing Expectations, 137-140

religion, 189-193

The Rescuer. See The Buddy

resistance, 31-36, 39

resources for finding a therapist, 221

Reticular Activating System (RAS), 155-156

roles

generally, 56

drama roles, 56-60

durable roles, 61-63

gender roles, 52

and patterns. See patterns

S

Satir, Virginia, 97-98

The Secret Debt, 78-80

security, 12, 23-24

self-disclosure, 110-115

selflessness, 133-136

self-regulation, 3, 110-115, 133-134, 228

Seligman, Martin, 156

separation, 36

sexual intimacy, 14-16, 65, 175-181

shame, 150

shared identity. See We (establishing)

shared meaning, 170-173

shared vision, 183-188

Six-Stage Change Cycle

generally, 11-14

You and Me (attaching), 14-18, 40-41

We (establishing), 18-22, 41

I and I (individuating), 22-24, 41-42

We/I Plateau (stabilizing), 24-28, 42-43

D-Factor (differentiating), 28-34, 43-44

Us or Me (integrating), 34-38, 44-45

assessing your stage, 45-47

challenges of, 38-40

Committed Couple Relationships Chart, 46

Is This Normal? Exercise, 47

lifespan illustration, 40-45

overlapping stages, 38

the soul, 195-200

speaking from your gut, 145

spirituality, 189-193

stabilizing (We/I Plateau), 24-28, 42-43

stewardship, 195-200

Stopping the Train, 119-125

styles. See conflict styles

Swan Story, 223-228

systemic thinking, 219

T

Thanks-for-Giving, 150-153

therapists, 218-221

thoughts

critical, 141-146

managing, 119-125

Three Positives, 155-158

top thoughts, 142-146

transgenerational accounting, 147-153

trauma history, 54-55

U

The Underfunctioning Partner. See The Baby; The Bully
The Un-Dreamers, 76-77
The Uneven Team, 67-69
Us or Me (integrating), 34-38, 44-45

V

values, 21, 183-188
Values Circle™, 183-184
The Victim. See The Baby
vision, 183-188

W

We (establishing), 18-22, 41
websites for finding a therapist, 221
We/I Plateau (stabilizing), 24-28, 42-43
What About You?, 207-211
Willard, Dallas, 102
work, 16, 21-26, 29-30

Y

You and Me (attaching), 14-18, 40-41

About the Author

Through two decades of experience, Jen Elmquist, MA, LMFT, has established the ability to motivate and transform individuals, couples, and audiences of all ages. By tapping into her background in communications, media, and marriage and family therapy, she develops and delivers innovative, outcome-based education to generate positive learning environments and enhanced relationships.

Jen's work also includes teaching, coaching, and therapy for adults and adolescents in clinical, corporate, and educational settings, along with a specialization in couple relationships. She is an AAMFT Nationally Approved Supervisor and an adjunct faculty member at Saint Mary's University, Graduate School of Marriage and Family Therapy in Minneapolis, Minnesota. She currently provides consulting services out of her private practice, Restoration Productions.

Residing between Chanhassen, Minnesota and San Diego, California, Jen enjoys time with her husband, Jess, their family, and two puppies.

Photography by Jamie Stoia, jstoiaportraitdesign.com